COMMODITY OPTIONS

COMMODITY OPTIONS:
SPECTACULAR PROFITS WITH LIMITED RISK

LARRY D. SPEARS

MARKETPLACE BOOKS

COLUMBIA, MARYLAND

This book, along with other books, are available at
discounts that make it realistic to provide them as
gifts to your customers, clients, and staff. For more
information on these long lasting, cost effective
premiums, please call John Boyer at 800.424.4550
or e-mail him at john@traderslibrary.com.

ISBN 1-883272-49-1

CONTENTS

"The future, the future! If only we knew the future!"

THE FIRST PERSON TO UTTER THAT LAMENT most likely lived in a cave – and the utterance was made in grunts. Man, you see, has been obsessed with the future since Adam and Eve stood outward bound at the gates of the Garden of Eden (or since the first anthropoid climbed down and left his fellow apes behind in the trees, if that's your predilection).

But, in spite of this obsession, man – even with all the advances of modern theory, science and technology – is still unable to change, or even accurately predict, the future.

Oh, it's not for a lack of trying. In fact, some men have found great success as a result of their efforts at this impossible task. The first man who figured out the moon was going to appear on a regular basis and predicted its arrival the following night attained mystical status in his tribe. He was held in awe and given a position of leadership.

And so it went, from the primitive witch doctors through the mystics of ancient Egypt to the Merlins of medieval England. The man who learned to play on his fellow man's fear, his longing to know the unknowable – and was smart enough to use that fear and longing to his own benefit – had power!

With the birth of modern science, a new kind of mystic emerged. This man did not so much predict the future as create it. He had the foresight to see what could be, but wasn't, and to do what could be done, but hadn't been. This man saw that the earth went around the sun, not vice versa – and then proved it. He saw that the world was round, not flat – and then proved it. He foresaw telescopes, steamships, railroads, automobiles, airplanes, computers, spaceships – and then worked to create them or inspired others to do so.

Where the old-style mystics had used fear to foster the impression they could see into the future, these new mystics used knowledge to turn the future into the things they could see.

Still, no one could – or can – predict the future. And this creates problems for us all – especially if we are investors, for all our best efforts today may be for naught if the future turns out differently than we expected. "The best laid schemes o'mice an' men..." as Robert Burns once wisely said.

What can we do? Most of us have neither the intelligence nor the resources to create the future. And few of us – the Joe Granvilles of the world notwithstanding – have a following large enough to mandate that our predictions come true. The pursuit of a perfect future is an exercise in utter futility. It is pure folly for even the best-informed investor to believe he will always be right. The best we can realistically do is make our bets and then hedge them in case Dame Fortune frowns on our efforts.

In this book we'll be talking about investment vehicles that can give us a sensible means to hedge our bets – and, if the future proves us right rather than wrong, to create truly spectacular profits as well. We'll explain exactly what these vehicles are, why and how they were developed, how they work, and how you can use them successfully for both hedging and limited-risk speculation.

So, if your pointy, star-covered hat has grown too big; if the pointer on your Ouija board is down to splinters; if your tarot cards are frayed and you've thrown your bones until they're worn smooth... If you've done all this and you're still not sure how to protect your financial future, read on.

FUTURES: THE CONCEPT AND THE REASONING

There are two kinds of options in the world of commodities: options on the actual physical commodities themselves, and options on commodity futures. In this book, we'll be dealing almost exclusively with the latter since, in just a few short years, they've become one of the hottest investment vehicles on the market.

Before we advance into a detailed discussion of options on commodity futures, however, it's essential that we understand commodity futures themselves. Almost everyone, of course, knows about commodities – they are simply the raw materials needed to produce a finished product, whether that product is bacon or bread or an airplane with aluminum skin.

That's a simple enough definition for anyone to grasp – and the concept of "futures contracts" is equally simple. Futures are merely contracts to buy or sell actual commodities at some future date. And, whether you're talking about pork bellies, wheat, corn, coffee, precious metals, Treasury securities, stock indices or whatever, the concept is the same.

A Basic Function of Good Business

Why is there a need for futures? The answer lies in the basic function of almost every business – which, as mentioned above, is to produce some kind of finished product and to do it in an orderly and profitable fashion. Futures facilitate orderly and profitable production by ensuring that the necessary raw materials are available when needed – and at a cost low enough to guarantee a profit.

For example, let's look at a baker. Assume the baker made loaves of bread which he sold for 50 cents each. His primary costs were flour and labor. If the wheat to make the flour cost 16 cents per loaf, the labor 14 cents, and other items a total of 10 cents, then the baker's cost was 40 cents. He was making 10 cents profit on each loaf, or a 25 percent return. Sounds like a nice business, no?

But then trouble struck. Hail wiped out half the year's wheat crop and the price of wheat doubled. Suddenly the baker's cost for flour was 32 cents. And, just as suddenly, instead of making a 25 percent profit on his 50-cent loaf, the baker was losing money. He had 56 cents in costs. In order to restore his 25 percent profit margin, he had to start charging 70 cents per loaf. Unfortunately, his chief competitor had stocked up on 16-cent flour right before the hail storm and could afford to still charge only 50 cents per loaf. What happened? Obviously, our poor baker went out of business.

This kind of risk obviously wasn't what people had in mind when they sank their dough into the baking business. But what could be done? A system was needed to ensure a steady flow of wheat at level, or at least predictable, prices.

Fortunately, one thing is forever certain when it comes to the pursuit of profit: when a system for something is needed, it will always be developed.

And the system in this case was futures!

The baker, knowing he would need to buy a certain amount of wheat in three months to continue making his flour, offered to buy a "futures contract" from the farmer. The baker agreed to pay the farmer one cent now. For this payment, the farmer promised to sell the baker wheat for his flour three months from now at a cost of 16 cents per loaf.

A Good Deal For Both Buyer & Seller

This was a good deal for both. The baker reduced his profit margin slightly by paying the penny now, but he ensured his supply of 16-cent wheat. And, the farmer got 17 cents for wheat he probably could have otherwise sold for only 16 cents.

Of course, there was another side of the coin. If the price of wheat went up, the farmer still had to sell it for 16 cents. He could possibly lose 4 or 5 cents in exchange for guaranteeing himself a 17-cent price. The baker would likewise lose money if the price of wheat went down due to an oversupply — he still had to pay 16 cents even if the market price had dipped to 12 cents. Both sides could lose, but all they could lose was possible extra profits. Neither could lose as badly as they might have without the agreement.

And, the uncertainty was taken out of the future for both parties.

Thus, that's what futures are all about – ensuring against that which you cannot predict. I won't go into the growth of the futures business in commodities, the establishment of the big trading markets, or the development of speculation because this really isn't a book about commodities.

It is instead a book about even further refinements in the art of ensuring against that which you cannot predict – and profiting handsomely when the predictions you do make come true. This is the potential commodity options offer – so let's find out more about them.

COMMODITY OPTIONS: A CHECKERED HISTORY

As I mentioned earlier, there are two kinds of commodity options: options on the actual physical commodities themselves, and options on commodity futures.

The former have been around for several centuries under a variety of names, ranging from privileges to bids to advance guarantees and other such antiquated terms. In their first life in the United States, back in the 1860s, options on agricultural commodities proved very popular. Soon, however, speculative excesses prompted widespread criticism of the options, and they became the target of constant complaints and frequent restrictions. Profits on them were severely taxed in the 1920s, and many were banned entirely in the 1930s, with more being forbidden throughout the '40s, '50s, and '60s until the U.S. market in commodity options ceased to exist.

Interest in the concept of commodity options refused to wane, however, and traders moved to overseas markets where they were still available. Unfortunately, disreputable dealers led investors into a series of frauds, scandals, and multimillion-dollar losses, and the resulting outcry prompted Congress to launch a major review of the entire commodity futures industry in the United States.

The result was the Commodity Futures Trading Commission Act of 1974, which created the Commodity Futures Trading Commission, or CFTC, an independent agency with responsibility for setting rules and governing actions of the American futures industry. The CFTC made one more stab at allowing organized trading of commodity options in the United States, but problems persisted even under the new tighter regulations, and all public sales of commodity options were eventually suspended. Congress reinforced this suspension with adoption of the Futures Trading Act of 1978, which man-

dated that a comprehensive set of regulations be developed

for options trading before any new trading was allowed.

A Change in Direction

Rather than beating what was rapidly becoming a dead

horse, the CFTC decided to look in a new direction. For

some time, London commodity markets had offered options

that could be exercised for futures contracts rather than for

the actual commodities themselves. Following this lead, the

CFTC decided to set up a pilot program involving options on

commodity futures – and, in late 1981, eight U.S. futures

exchanges sought permission to trade in these options.

In addition, the major security exchanges (some of which

had been trading in stock options since the early '70s) decid-

ed they wanted to offer options on various "paper commodi-

ties," such as Treasury bills, certificates of deposit and foreign currencies. The Securities and Exchange Commission (SEC), which governs these exchanges, worked out regulations for this trading, agreeing to give the CFTC jurisdiction over all security-based futures options while retaining control of options on actual securities.

Congress gave its stamp of approval to the entire regulatory arrangement in 1982, and the first futures options – for sugar, gold and Treasury bonds -began trading late that year. At the same time, trading in SEC-regulated options on actual T-bills, Treasury notes, Treasury bonds and certain securities also started.

Interest in these new vehicles rose quickly. Trading in options on the Standard & Poor's 500 Index futures contract and the New York Stock Exchange Index futures contract began in 1983, as did cash-settled options on five actual stock indices – the S&P 500, S&P 100, American

Stock Exchange Major Market Index, American Stock Exchange Market Value Index, and the NYSE Composite Index. In 1984, options on futures contracts representing soybeans, wheat, cotton, live cattle, silver, and the German mark were introduced.

There are also cash-settled options on a variety of other stock indices, including the Value Line Index; an over-the-counter stock index; a gold/silver index; and various stock groups such as oil, technology, computers, and transportation. Options on actual currencies have also been added for the British pound, Canadian dollar, French franc, Swiss franc, and Japanese yen. In addition, interest-rate options based on Eurodollars and various U.S. Treasury issues are traded.

To the ranks of derivatives on futures contracts have been added options on two more types of wheat and the two major soybean products; options on corn and canola; contracts for live hogs, pork bellies, and feeder cattle; options on copper and lumber; another silver contract; options on 10-year Treasury notes, Eurodollars, and a municipal bond index; options on the British pound, Swiss franc, japanese yen, Canadian dollar, and on a U.S. dollar index; contracts on the S&P 100 Stock Index and NYSE Composite Index; options on cocoa, coffee, and orange juice; and contracts on crude oil, heating oil, and unleaded gasoline.

Thus, you can see that for a market barely two decades old, the commodity options field has become both popular and diverse. And, still more options on both futures contracts and actual commodities have been proposed.

What all this means, in one word, is opportunity – but only if you understand these youthful vehicles and can learn to use them properly. That's what this book is all about – teaching you to take advantage of this opportunity. Before we go on, however, I want to make sure you'll fully compre-

hend the strategies we'll be discussing, so I'm going to take

a few pages to define and explain the unique terminology of

commodity futures and options.

GLOSSARY

Futures and options have a language all their own. For that reason I feel it's important to have the glossary at the front of this book, rather than at the back as is customary. Please take a few minutes to familiarize yourself with the terms defined here – you'll increase your understanding of the rest of the book immensely.

ASSIGNMENT — The notice given to the writer of an option informing him that the option has been exercised by the buyer.

AT-THE-MONEY — When the exercise, or strike, price of an option is equal to the current market price of the underlying commodity or futures contract.

BEAR — An investor who thinks that the price of a commodity underlying a futures contract is heading down and, therefore, the price of those futures contracts will also decline. A "bear market" is a general downward trend in a market or specific group, such as agricultural commodities. A bear market is ideal for put buyers or call writers, as well as traders of call spreads.

BULL — An investor who thinks that the price of a commodity underlying a futures contract is going to rise and, therefore, the price of those futures contracts will also increase. A "bull market" is a general upward trend in all commodity prices or in the prices of a specific group, such as precious metals. A bull market is ideal for call buyers or put writers, as well as put spreads.

BUYER — An investor who purchases an option, either a call or put, thus establishing a "long" position. The buyer is also referred to as the purchaser or holder of an option.

CALENDAR SPREAD — An options play involving the purchase and sale of two option contracts of the same type and strike price, but with different expiration dates.

CALL — An option giving the purchaser the right to BUY a specific commodity or futures contract at a designated price for a limited period of time (until the expiration date).

CALL FOR DELIVERY — Demand that the seller of a call deliver the futures contract at the price specified by that call.

CHARTING — The use of charts and graphs in the technical analysis of commodity price trends, futures prices, volume, etc.

CLASS OF OPTIONS — All call options — or all put options — covering the same underlying futures contract. In the case of currencies, stock indices, and Treasury securities that have "serial" options, the option class can include contracts with differing expiration dates.

CLEARING ORGANIZATION —An organization associated with a futures exchange that is responsible for the settlement of all transactions involving futures or options traded on that exchange. The clearing organization serves as the buyer to all sellers and the seller to all buyers, thus eliminating the need to directly match up buyers and sellers. This makes for a more orderly market and increases liquidity in the market.

CLOSING PRICE —The final price at which a security of any kind was traded during the market day.

CLOSING TRANSACTION —The purchase or sale of an option to get out of a previously established position — i.e., buying back an option identical to one written earlier, or selling an option identical to one purchased earlier.

COMBINATION —A position involving either the purchase or sale of both calls and puts on the same underlying futures contract.

COMMODITY FUTURES TRADING COMMISSION(CFTC) —The U.S. government agency responsible for regulation of trading in commodity futures and options.

CONTRACT — An agreement established when one person buys an option and another person sells the same option. The two transactions combined create a "contract."

CORRECTION — A minor market move against the established trend.

COVER-ED — Any position that carries no margin requirement because you own an offsetting position. In the case of commodity options, you can cover the sale of a call by owning the underlying futures contract or by buying cans of longer term or nearer-to-the-money strike price; you can cover the sale of a put by being short the underlying futures contract.

EXCHANGE MINIMUM —The smallest amount of equity required by an exchange to open or maintain a futures or option position. Brokerage firms also have "house minimums" which must be at least as strict as the exchange minimum, but which usually are more restrictive.

EXERCISE —An action by the holder of an option demanding fulfillment of the terms of that option — i.e., an action by a call holder demanding delivery of the underlying futures contract at the stated price, or an action by a put holder demanding that delivery of the underlying futures contract be taken at the stated price.

EXERCISE PRICE —The price at which a call buyer can buy the underlying futures contract, or at which a put buyer can sell the underlying contract. Also known as the "strike price."

EXPIRATION DATE —The last day on which an option can be exercised. Unlike stock options (and options on most index futures), most options on futures are referred to by the delivery month of the underlying futures contract, rather than by the month in which they actually expire. For example, "a July 13-cent sugar call" expires on the second Friday of June, but it is described as a July option because it calls for delivery of a July sugar futures contract. An option that is not exercised or offset by a closing transaction on or before the expiration date becomes null and void.

FAIR VALUE —An options fair value is the price at which the buyer pays a premium to the seller sufficient that both parties might expect to break even (excluding commissions and fees). Fair value is a theoretical concept, thus actual option prices may vary significantly from that "ideal" price.

FUTURES CONTRACT —A futures contract is a promise to make or take delivery of a specified commodity at a specified price at some future date. The term "futures contract" refers only to those contracts traded on a commodity exchange.

GRANTOR — A person who sells an option, also called seller or writer.

HEDGE — A position in which you buy a commodity, futures contract or option and offset that position with other futures or options in order to protect against all or some portion of your possible loss.

HORIZONTAL SPREAD — See calendar spread.

IN-THE-MONEY OPTION —A call with a striking price below the current market price of the underlying futures contract, or a put with a striking price above the current market price of the underlying futures contract. An option two or three striking prices below (in the case of a call) or above (in the case of a put) the current market price is said to be "deep in the money." In-the-money options are said to have "intrinsic," or real value, as opposed to only "time" value.

INTRINSIC VALUE —The actual dollar value of the difference between an options strike price and the current market value of the underlying futures contract.

LEVERAGE —The use of a small amount of money to control a security of much greater value so that a small change in the price of the underlying security produces a much higher percentage gain on the actual sum invested. Futures contracts and options are noted for the high leverage they offer.

LIMIT ORDER — An order to buy or sell a security specifying a minimum or maximum price for the transaction.

LIMITED RISK — A position in which the maximum possible loss can be calculated before it is entered into.

LIQUIDATE — Close out a security position. If a futures contract price moves adversely to a position you hold and you fail to supply the required margin money to maintain the position, the broker or exchange may sell your position in what is known as a "forced liquidation."

LIQUIDITY —The extent to which there is a market for a given security or investment. Real estate is difficult to sell and therefore has low liquidity, while there is a ready market for stocks, giving them high liquidity. The liquidity in a futures contract or option can be gauged by the amount of open interest in the particular contract or option.

LONG — Designation for a market position that has been established through "purchase" of a futures contract or option without any offsetting sale of a similar contract or option.

MAINTENANCE CALL — A demand from the exchange or brokerage firm that you put up more money in order to maintain a position. Such a call is prompted by a move in the price of the security in the opposite direction from what you had expected.

MARGIN — Money or securities that must be deposited in your brokerage account to help ensure that you will fulfill the terms of your futures or option contracts.

MARGIN ACCOUNT — A brokerage account in which you are allowed to take positions without fully paying for them-in essence borrowing a part of the purchase price from the broker. The exact amounts that can be borrowed are regulated by the government, securities exchanges, and the brokerage firm.

MARGIN CALL — A demand from the exchange or brokerage firm that you put up additional money in order to maintain the required equity necessary to hold a position you previously entered into.

MARK-TO-MARKET —The valuation of any open position at the end of a trading day to assess the requirement for more (or less) margin to maintain a position that has lost (or gained) value.

MARKET ORDER — An order to purchase or sell a security at the best available price at the time the order reaches the trading floor of the security exchange.

MATURITY — The date an option expires.

NAKED OPTION — A exposed position — i.e., one in which you sell an option without controlling the underlying futures contract or owning an offsetting option.

NATIONAL FUTURES ASSOCIATION (NFA) — An organization of futures exchanges, commodity brokerage firms, institutional (fund) traders and trading advisers that serves as a self-regulating body for the futures industry. It responds to complaints by retail customers and oversees arbitration efforts generally referred to as the NFA.

OPEN INTEREST — The total number of futures contracts or options outstanding at a given time. It takes both an original purchase transaction and an original sale transaction to create an open interest of one contract; thus the open interest is equal to the total number of long or short positions in the market at a given time.

OPENING TRANSACTION — A transaction in which an investor establishes a long position by buying an option or a short position by writing an option.

OPTION —A contract which gives the holder the right to purchase (call) or sell (put) the underlying security or futures contract at a specific price within a set period of time.

OUT-OF-THE-MONEY OPTION —A call with a strike price higher than the current market price of the underlying futures contract, or a put with a strike price lower than the current market price of the underlying futures contract.

OVERBOUGHT — A general condition in a market in which prices have risen too high too quickly. May also refer to prices for a specific security. The opposite condition, in which prices for the market in general or for a specific security have fallen too far too quickly, is called "oversold."

PARTIALLY COVERED —A position in which options are sold and less than the equivalent amount of underlying futures contracts or offsetting options is owned.

PREMIUM —The amount of money paid by the buyer of an option for that option, usually quoted in units of the underlying commodity (for example, a quoted premium of 38 cents on a May $6.00 soybean call would represent 38 cents per bushel, or a total of $1,900 for the call on a 5,000-bushel May futures contract). The premium can be composed of two parts, one representing intrinsic value and the other representing the value of the time remaining before the option expires — or, in the case of out-of-the-money options, it can consist of time value only. The premium is kept by the seller regardless of whether the option is exercised or not.

PROFIT ZONE — A price range, which can be predetermined, within which an option combination will produce a gain.

PUT — An option giving the purchaser the right to SELL a specific security, commodity, or futures contract at a designated price for a specified period of time.

QUOTE —The highest price a buyer is offering for a security and the lowest price at which someone is willing to sell the same security at any given time. Also called the "bid price" and "asked price," respectively. Generally, the two prices are slightly different, with the difference being known as the "bid-ask spread."

RISK-REWARD RATIO —The relation between the possible loss and the possible profit on a given position.

SELLING SHORT — Description for an opening sale transaction in which you sell a security without having owned it.

SERIES OF OPTIONS — Options of the same class having the same strike price and expiration date.

SHORT — A position in which you are a seller of a specific option or futures contract.

SPREAD —A position in which options are both bought and sold on the same underlying futures contract. The expiration dates and striking prices may be the same or different. See "combination."

SPREAD ORDER. — An order to position both sides of a spread at the same time without regard to the actual price of each side, but with the difference between the two prices specified. For example, rather than trying to buy a May $5.50 soybean call at exactly 28 cents per bushel and sell a May $5.75 soybean call option at exactly 12 cents per bushel, you would tell the broker to "buy a $5.50 soybean call and sell a $5.75 soybean call at a spread of 16 cents or better." The broker could then fill the order at any combination of individual -option prices that yielded a debit of 16 cents or less.

STABILITY —The extent to which a commodity or security is expected to stay around the same price.

STOP ORDER —An order to buy or sell a security that goes into effect only when the price of the security reaches a set level. Often used to limit losses when a commodity price moves adversely to an existing position you hold. Also referred to as a stop-loss order.

STRADDLE — A position in which you buy or sell both a put and a can with the same striking price and the same expiration date on the same underlying futures contract.

STRIKE (OR STRIKING) PRICE — See exercise price.

TIME VALUE —The portion of an option premium that is paid for the time remaining until the option expires. "Intrinsic value" or "real value" is that part of the premium reflecting how much an option is "in the money."

UNCOVERED OPTION — See "naked option."

UNDERLYING COMMODITY —The commodity or futures contract an option buyer has the right to purchase or sell under the terms of the option. For example, a "December $2.50 corn call" would give the buyer the right to buy one December corn futures contract calling for delivery of 5,000 bushels of corn at a price of $2.50 a bushel.

VERTICAL SPREAD — A combination involving the purchase and sale of two options of the same type with the same expiration date, but with different strike prices.

VOLATILITY —The degree to which a security is likely to move up or down from its current price. Recent volatility is a major factor in determining the amount of time value appropriate in the premium of a given option.

WRITING AN OPTION —Writing is simply another term for "selling." It is called writing because options are intangible and the seller of an option actually "creates" it at the time he offers it for sale.

If you are an experienced veteran of futures trading, or even an occasional participant in the commodity markets, most of these terms are probably already familiar to you. For those of you who have yet to try your hand at futures or options, however, an understanding of the language of the markets will prove invaluable as you learn about the opportunities these vehicles can offer in your investment program.

PART ONE

Taking Advantage of How Options on Futures Work

VERSATILE TOOLS TO MEET EVERY INVESTOR'S NEEDS

If you're a farmer, a manufacturer, a banker, or any of dozens of other professionals actively engaged in the use of commodities and commodity futures, the merits of options on futures are probably already quite apparent to you. They offer additional hedging opportunities — often at a much lower cost than traditional hedging techniques — as well as a variety of new strategies for enhancing profits.

As tools for managing risk, locking in gains, and creating additional profits, options on futures have also quickly gained a valued spot in the portfolios of experienced futures traders and commodity speculators.

The most exciting aspect of options on futures, however, is not their usefulness to businessmen, veteran traders, or experienced speculators. It is the opportunity they offer to the average investor — the investor who, until now, has been reluctant to buy or sell futures contracts because the fear of unlimited risk outweighed all the promises of enormous profit.

Futures, you see, are double-edged swords. They offer tremendous leverage, allowing you to control commodities worth thousands of dollars by putting up only a few hundred dollars in margin money. If you are right, and the price of the commodity moves the way you expect, you can multiply your original investment by 10, 20, even 100 times.

But, just as there is no limit to the profits you can make if you are right, there is no limit on the losses you can suffer if you are wrong. You could put up $500 to secure a futures position and wind up losing not just that $500, but $5,000 — or more — if the market moved against you quickly and dramatically.

In addition, futures represent one-to-one contracts. For every buyer, there must be a seller — and for every winner, there must be a loser. Trading futures is not like buying stocks, where everyone can profit when the market goes up. Repeated research has shown that 10 percent of the traders in futures make 90 percent of the profits, and that about 85 percent of the people who trade in commodities wind up losing money. Since the livelihood of the farmers, businessmen, and professional traders depend on their success in these markets, you can be sure that they dominate the list of winners, leaving everyone else in the loser's column.

For these reasons alone, the vast majority of typical investors have heeded the repeated warnings by conservative investment advisors that "futures trading is for experienced professionals only — much too dangerous for the average person."

But, with options on futures — specifically "call" options and "put" options — it's a different story entirely. Someone once described the ideal investment vehicle as one that offers unlimited profit potential, but has limited and defined risk.

And that's exactly what options do!

Assume that you think the price of a commodity is about to move up. If you buy an option — in this case a "call" — on the futures contract for that commodity, and are right, your profits will continue to increase as long as the price of the commodity continues to rise. But, if you are wrong, the absolute maximum you can lose is the amount you paid for the option in the first place.

"Put" options work exactly the opposite. If you anticipated a big downward move in the price of a particular commodity, you'd purchase one or more puts, which would give you the right to "sell" futures contracts on the commodity. If you're right, again big profits; and if you're wrong, the most you lose is the original cost of the options (plus transaction costs, of course).

Options offer maximum leverage

We're not talking about small profits either. Since each option represents the right (though not the obligation) to buy or sell an actual futures contract, you still have the same tremendous leverage you'd get if you bought the futures contract outright. In other words, you once again control thousands of dollars worth of a commodity even though you may have paid only several hundred dollars for the option.

The key difference between options and actual futures contracts for purposes of defining risk lies in that word "obligation" in the paragraph above. With futures, you have the obligation to fulfill the terms of the contract, whether the price goes for you or against you —and this means you must accept big losses as well as big gains. But, with options, you have no obligation to buy the futures contract if prices go against you — you can simply let the option expire and forfeit the small amount you paid for it. (This may seem a bit nebulous right now, but I'll explain it fully with examples when we get into the discussion of option strategies.)

And that's just the beginning — buying puts and calls is only the most basic of strategies involving options. Options can be used effectively in virtually any market environment. Some strategies are well suited to markets in which prices are highly volatile, while others provide opportunities in markets in which there is little expectation of price movement in either direction. In other words, options on futures expand your financial choices and enable you to have greater flexibility. And, in today's competitive investment markets, the versatile investor clearly enjoys a significant advantage — if not a unique ability to survive.

Say, for example, that you really have no conviction about the way the market for a particular commodity may move. Often the price levels of options are such that you have the opportunity to earn a higher-than-market rate of return on capital by "selling" (also referred to as "granting" or "writing") options. The return is derived from the money — or "premium" — that the option buyer pays you for the option. A word of warning, though, unlike the limited risk gained by an option buyer, a seller's potential loss may exceed the premium he receives.

STRATEGIES FOR EVERY INVESTMENT GOAL

Options can also be traded in conjunction with either futures contracts or other options. Buying or writing options in combination with futures offers a variety of potentially attractive strategies — including techniques for realizing speculative profits, generating cash flow, limiting market risks, and "insuring" unrealized profits. And using options in conjunction with other options can create "spread" or "combination" positions that are virtually risk-free. All of these strategies can be tailored to both your individual investment goals and to changing market conditions.

So, let's get on with a more detailed look at some of the strategies and trading techniques — and the arithmetic involved. Once you get the hang of it, you should be able to calculate just how options on futures can enhance your own investment program — and open up new areas of potential profit.

Back in the introduction, I explained briefly the reasoning behind futures. Before you can fully understand how options on futures work, though, we need to take a brief look at exactly how a futures contract is structured and how profits and losses are generated.

As outlined earlier, a futures contract is simply a contract between two people — a buyer and seller — involving a set amount of a given commodity, a price for that commodity, and a specified time and place for the delivery of the commodity. The quantity and quality of the commodity, as well as acceptable dates for delivery, are fixed by the various commodity exchanges. The selling price of the commodity is determined in the competitive marketplace at the time the contract is established. Theoretically, at any given time, the futures price should reflect not only the current price for the underlying commodity, but also the best available information on expected supply and demand for it in the future, as well as information on peripheral factors such as carrying charges (the cost of storing the commodity prior to delivery, as well as the interest charge or opportunity risk involved in tying up money in the commodity).

Thus, as the outlook for the actual commodity changes, so do prices on futures representing that commodity. Because futures prices track the value of the actual commodity, commercial firms seeking price protection (as well as investors seeking profits) are able to buy and sell futures contracts rather than having to buy, store, and deliver the commodity itself. The advantages are obvious: the initial cost is smaller; there's a continuous, competitive, and liquid marketplace; and regulation by the CFTC, futures exchanges, and futures clearing organizations assures the financial integrity of each deal.

I mentioned the tremendous leverage available in futures earlier, and that leverage is a major attraction for investors. Once again, a futures transaction does not require full advance payment for the commodi-ty represented by the contract. In other words, if you buy a futures contract for 100 ounces of gold on the New York Commodity Exchange (COMEX), you do not have to pay $33,200 (the current cash value of 100 ounces of gold). You only have to put up a "margin" deposit, which serves as a good-faith guarantee that you will fulfill the obligations created by the contract you bought. (The actual margin requirements vary from exchange to exchange and from broker to broker, and also change frequently. The figures supplied in this book will be for purposes of illustration only; you should check with your broker to find the exact requirements before entering into any futures contract.)

A 500% profit

Let's say that gold is selling for $335 an ounce and you buy a gold futures contract calling for delivery of 100 troy ounces of gold in October at a price of $340 an ounce (futures for gold carry a small time premium reflecting storage and carrying costs over the life of the contract).

You put up $ 1,000 as a margin deposit — that's your only cash commitment so long as the price of gold doesn't move down. (If it does, you might get a "margin call" asking you to put up more money to ensure that you'll cover your loss, but we'll assume that doesn't happen.)

Let's assume that, by October, gold rises in price to $390 an ounce. The person who sold the futures contract must deliver 100 ounces of gold to you, charging you only $340 an ounce. (Actually, most futures contracts are never carried to the point of delivery, but rather are off-set, or sold, for the cash equivalent value of the actual commodity.)

You pay out $34,000 and immediately resell the gold at its current market value of $39,000 (100 ounces x $390/ounce = $39,000), pocketing a $5,000 profit. Thus, you have a 500 percent return on your initial cash commitment of $1,000 (which, by the way, you still have, since it was only a deposit). Had you actually bought 100 ounces of physical gold instead of buying a futures contract, you would have had to pay the full $33,500 cost up front (remember, the futures contract carried a $5 an ounce premium). Selling at $39,000, you would have made a profit of $5,500, but your return on investment would have been just 16.4 percent — not 500 percent.

That's leverage — and it can be a powerful investment tool.

Leverage works both ways

Don't forget, as we explained earlier, that leverage can work both ways -especially with futures. Had gold gone down -say to $290 an ounce — you could have lost not only your entire $1,000 margin deposit, but $4,000 more (assuming you met all the margin calls from your broker). Thus your loss would have been 500 percent.

This high level of risk with futures brings us back to the major advantage offered by options on futures — they let you limit that risk with virtually no reduction in the profit potential. Once you plop down your cash and buy an option, you are never subject to a margin call. Even if you are wrong, your maximum loss is the one-time-only cost of the option premium.

Using the same example, let's examine the difference. Instead of buying an October gold futures contract, you buy a call option that gives you the right to buy an October gold futures contract calling for delivery of gold at $340 an ounce. You pay the seller of the option a premium of $1,000 ($10 an ounce is a reasonable premium in our example though premiums vary widely depending on the current price of the commodity and the length of time covered by the option).

Again, gold rises to $390 an ounce. You exercise your call (what you'd actually do in most cases is just sell the call and accept your profit in cash rather than buying the futures contract and calling for delivery). Once the person who sold the call delivers the futures contract, you again take delivery of the gold, paying $34,000, and immediately sell it, collecting the current market value of $39,000.

This time your profit is $4,000 — $5,000 gain on the gold, minus the $1,000 you paid for the call option (and you did pay it; with options you are NOT just putting up a deposit). Thus, you have a gain of 400 percent on your initial investment.

"Wait a minute!" you say. "Why would I want to use options instead of futures if I'm going to reduce my profit from 500 percent to 400 percent?"

The answer is quite simple once you again look at the other possibility — that you might be wrong. Remember, when you bought the futures contract, you were obligated to fulfill the terms even if the price went against you. In our example, when gold dropped to $290 an ounce, you lost $5,000, or 500 percent on your initial investment. But, with an option, you don't have that worry. If gold goes to $290 an ounce, you obviously don't want to exercise your option to buy a futures contract calling for delivery at $340 an ounce. So, you simply sell the option at a loss or let it expire worthless.

The price you pay to limit risk

Either way, your maximum possible loss is the original $1,000 you paid as a premium — a loss that was fully defined and limited the day you bought the option. Instead of losing 500 percent of your original investment, as you would have with the futures contract in our example, you can never lose more than 100 percent of the premium you pay for the option.

Thus, the slight reduction in potential profit — in our example, from a 500 percent gain to a 400 percent gain — is the price you pay for having an absolute limit on the amount you can lose if you're wrong.

This is not to suggest that options should be considered a total substitute for futures. Both futures and options offer certain strong advantages for specific investors in certain situations. In fact, most knowledgeable investors have learned they can best achieve their goals and control their risks by using a combination of both options and futures.

THE BASIC ELEMENTS OF OPTIONS

Just in case you skipped through the glossary and haven't gotten all the basics regarding options on futures from our discussion so far, I'm going to repeat the definitions and further explain some of the basic elements before we go on to strategies.

A call option gives the buyer the right (but not the obligation) to purchase a specific futures contract at a specified price for a specific period of time.

For example, a July 12-cent sugar call would give the purchaser the right to buy one July sugar futures contract calling for delivery of sugar at a price of 12 cents a pound at any time between the date of purchase and the date the option expired. (You will note that options are described in terms of the futures contracts they represent. Thus, you might encounter "a July 12-cent sugar call" or "an October $340 gold call," even though these respective options actually expire early in June and September.)

A put option gives the buyer the right (but not the obligation) to sell a specific futures contract at a specified price for a specific period of time.

For example, an August 75 cent live cattle put would give the purchaser the right to sell one August cattle futures contract calling for delivery of live cattle at a price of 75 cents a pound any time between the date it was purchased and the date it expired.

The price for which a futures contract can be bought (in the case of a call) or sold (in the case of a put) is called the options strike price or exercise price.

The date an option expires (in other words, the date after which it can no longer be exercised), is the options expiration date.

Bear in mind one very important point about the quoted expiration date: the option date refers to the futures contract delivery month, NOT to the month in which the option actually expires. For example, a May option on crude oil is an option to buy or sell a May crude oil futures contract. The option itself expires on a specified date during the preceding month — in the case of crude oil options, the expiration date is the second Friday of the month preceding the stated futures month. Thus, our May crude oil option would expire at the close of trading on the second Friday of April, and an October crude oil option would expire on the second Friday of September, etc.

Be absolutely certain you know precisely when an option expires before you buy or sell it (holidays, such as good Friday, Thanksgiving, or Christmas may sometimes alter the expiration date). To help you out, a list of the expiration dates for some of the most commonly traded options on commodity futures follows:

OPTION   EXPIRATION DATE

Corn   The first Friday at least 10 business days prior to the first delivery notice day on the futures contract.★

Soybeans The first Friday at least 10 business days prior to the first delivery notice day on the futures contract.★

Cotton   The first Friday of the month prior to the futures contract delivery month.

Wheat   The first Friday at least 10 business days prior to the first delivery notice day on the futures contract.★

Sugar   The second Friday of the month preceding the futures contract delivery month.

Live Cattle The fourth business day prior to the first business day of the futures contract delivery month.

Live Hogs The fourth business day prior to the first business day of the futures contract delivery month.

Currencies The second Friday preceding the third Wednesday of the option expiration month.

(NOTE: Currencies have what are known as "serial" options, meaning an option is available expiring in every month, even if it is not a contract delivery month for the underlying future. For example, there are currency options expiring January, February and March, but all three call for delivery of the March currency futures contract.)

Gold   The second Friday of the month preceding the futures contract delivery month.

Silver   The second Friday of the month preceding the futures contract delivery month.

Crude Oil The second Friday of the month preceding the futures contract delivery month.

T-Bonds   The third Friday of the month preceding the futures contract delivery month.

NYSE   The business day prior to the last business day of the Composite futures contract delivery month. (These options expire at Index the same time as the futures, which are settled in cash come due for delivery.)

S&P 500   The third Friday of the option expiration month for serial options expiring in non-delivery months and the third Thursday of the futures contract delivery month. (Once again, serial options are available on the stock index futures. Thus, options expiring in October, November and December all call for delivery of the December futures contract.)

The notice day is the date on which the commodity clearing house informs the folder of a futures contract that the underlying commodity is ready for delivery. The holder must then either offset his contract or prepare to take delivery of the actual commodity.

THE 'PREMIUM' ON OPTIONS

One other important term relating to options is premium. The premium is the sum of money paid by the buyer of an option to the seller of an option in exchange for the rights granted by the option.

Premiums are determined through competition between buyers and sellers and their representatives on the trading floor of the futures exchanges. In other words, the premium on any given option at any given time is the market's assessment of what a particular option is worth at that exact time.

Understanding premiums is extremely important because, in a very real sense, the premium is what options trading is all about. Because the premium is actually the "market price" of an option at a given time, the profitability of most option trading strategies depends almost entirely on increases or decreases in the size of the premium.

For this reason, before you attempt to trade in options you should understand at least the fundamentals — if not the various sophisticated theoretical models and mathematical formulae — regarding how option premiums are determined and what factors influence them. (A comprehensive discussion of the various theories involving option premium behavior is beyond the range of this book alone as since entire books have been devoted to that subject alone. However, if you have a strong interest — and mathematical background — your broker or local librarian should be able to steer you in the direction of some of these books and studies.)

What you definitely should know — and remember — about option premiums is that they are determined by supply and demand, by the bids of prospective buyers and the demands of prospective sellers. In other words, option premiums must be low enough to entice potential buyers into purchasing the options and high enough to induce potential sellers to actually sell them.

One of the main responsibilities of an options exchange is to provide the facilities and establish the trading rules needed to assure that such a "middle ground" between seller and buyer can be reached in a relatively quick and efficient manner.

Two factors determine the premium

What buyers will actually pay for a particular option and what sellers will finally accept as payment for "writing" that option depends on two major factors: the options intrinsic value, and its time value. Let's take a look at both of these important variables through which the price, or premium, of an option is determined.

THE INTRINSIC VALUE OF AN OPTION

An options intrinsic value, if it has any, is based on the actual cash difference between its strike price and the current futures price. If an option would bring in cash if exercised — in other words, if it is "in the money" — then it is said to have intrinsic value. Call options, then, have intrinsic value when the actual futures price is above the strike price of the call. Let's look at an example:

A July corn call option has a strike price of $2.40 a bushel. If the July futures price is currently $2.45 a bushel, the call option has an intrinsic value of 5 cents a bushel — the difference between the $2.40 strike price and the $2.45 actual price. Such an option would be "in the money" by 5 cents a bushel, and the entire option contract would have a real, or intrinsic, value of $250 (5 cents x 5,000 bushels, the amount represented by a standard Chicago Board of Trade corn futures contract).

If the July futures price happened to be only $2.35 a bushel, then the July $2.40 corn call would be "out of the money" by 5 cents a bushel and the call would have no intrinsic value. In other words, any premium on the option would be solely a factor of the time remaining until the option expired.

In fact, different options on the same futures contract are probably most commonly referred to according to the level of their strike price relative to the actual futures price. In the case of calls, the terminology goes like this:

■ If the July corn futures price is $2.40, a July $2.50 corn call is said to be out of the money, meaning you would receive nothing if it were exercised.

■ If the July corn futures price is $2.50, a July $2.50 corn call is said to be at the money — an improved situation, though you would still receive nothing if the call were exercised.

■ If the July corn futures price is $2.60, a July $2.50 corn call is said to be in the money, meaning it would have 10 cents worth of intrinsic value — value you would receive if it were exercised.

The same definitions apply to all calls on futures, whether we are talking about October 12-cent sugar calls or December $350 gold options — if the calls strike price is below the futures price, it is "in the money," and if its strike price is above the futures price, it is "out of the money." Conversely, a put has intrinsic value only if the current futures price is below the options strike price. Thus, a July corn put option with a strike price of $2.50 a bushel would be in the money if the July futures price was $2.45 a bushel and out of the money if the July corn futures price was $2.55 a bushel. Applying the same terms to puts that we outlined above for calls, we get a situation that looks like this:

■ If the July corn futures price is $2.60, a July $2.50 corn put is said to be out of the money, meaning you would receive nothing if it were exercised.

■ If the July corn futures price Is $2.50, a July $2.50 corn put is said to be at the money — an improved situation, though it would still have no intrinsic value, meaning you'd get nothing if the put were exercised.

■ If the July corn futures price is $2.40, a July $2.50 corn put is said to be in the money, meaning it would have 10 cents worth of intrinsic value — value you would receive if it were exercised.

As you probably figured out from the above examples, an option with a strike price the same as the current futures price — whether it is a can or a put is described as an at-the-money option.

The premium on any given option — even if it has only one day of life left, will almost always equal or exceed its current intrinsic value. Otherwise, the option would have a market value below its real value and shrewd traders (called arbitraguers) with lots of money would buy up as many of these discounted options as possible and exercise them for the few pennies difference in price. Thus, with July corn at $2.55 a bushel, our July $2.50 call would most likely carry a premium of at least 51/2 cents, or $275, for the full 5,000-bushel contract. Likewise, a July $2.60 put would also probably carry a premium of 51/2 cents.

Time value considerations

Even if an option doesn't have intrinsic value, it still has a premium — and without intrinsic value, the premium can reflect only one thing: the time value of the option. Thus, with out-of-the-money options, the premium is always merely time value.

But what exactly is time value? Simply put, in the case of out-of-the-money options, it is the amount buyers are willing to pay on the chance that, at some time before the option expires, the price of the underlying futures contract will move enough to make the option profitable to exercise. In the case of in-the-money options — those with intrinsic value — the time value is the extra amount buyers are willing to risk in hopes the option will move deeper into the money.

OPTIONS ARE 'WASTING ASSETS'

Since all options eventually expire — in other words, reach a date after which they are worthless — they are often referred to as "wasting assets." This means that, all else being equal, an option should — and nearly always does — have less and less time value as it approaches its expiration date. It also means that an option a long way out of the money win have less time value than an otherwise identical option that's only a little bit out of the money. This is because the price of the underlying future must move much further in the same amount of time in order for the "deep" out-of-the-money option to gain any intrinsic value. Since the odds against this happening are greater, the risk is also greater and buyers are willing to pay less for the option.

A number of other factors also influence the size of option premiums, the most important one being the historic price volatility of the underlying commodity. Option premiums on futures contracts representing commodities that experience frequent, sharp price movements are generally higher than premiums on seemingly identical options on commodities with a history of stable prices.

Another factor in the size of premiums is the trend of commodity prices in general — calls carry higher premiums when the market is moving up, while put premiums rise when the market is moving down. Still another factor is the current level of interest rates, since higher market rates give investors more alternatives for achieving high. returns with lower risk.

In summary, then, the key factors influencing the premium of options on commodity futures — or order of importance — are:

- The proximity of the option strike price to the actual price of the underlying futures contract.

- The amount of time remaining before the option expires.

- The price volatility of the commodity underlying the futures contract.

- The supply of and demand for options as influenced by the direction of the trend in the market in general.

- The current level of interest rates.

There is one other aspect of option premiums that needs to be discussed before we move on — how they change relative to changes in the price of the underlying futures contract.

As a general rule, an increase in the underlying futures price will result in a smaller increase in the premium of a related call and a smaller decrease in the price of a related put. Conversely, a decrease in the underlying futures price win result in a smaller decrease in the premium of a related call and a smaller increase in the price of a related put. In other words, because of the time element and other factors affecting options, they rarely move cent for cent or dollar for dollar with the underlying futures contract. The one exception to this rule involves options that are deep, deep in the money — a $260 gold can, for example, would probably go up on a dollar-for-dollar basis with the underlying futures price once that price got to $300 or so.

In fact, different options on the same commodity futures contract win react differently to a change in the price of that futures contract.

An out-of-the-money option with one month of life remaining will move much less in reaction to a move in the underlying commodity price than win one with, say, six months of life remaining. For example, if gold moves from $345 an ounce to $355 an ounce in early July, the price of a December $360 gold futures call will move much more in response than will the price of an August $360 gold futures call. The reason is that the August option has only a few days of life left — meaning gold has only a few days to move up past $360 — while the

December call still has several months in which gold can continue to move upward.

On the other hand, an in-the-money option with less time remaining until expiration will probably move more in price than an in-the-money option of longer term, even though both options have the same amount of intrinsic value. The reason is that the time value makes up a much bigger percentage of the total premium of the longer-term option, and that time value win decrease as the option moves deeper into the money. For example, if gold was at $355 an ounce in late June, the August $340 gold call might have a premium of $17 ($15 intrinsic value, $2 time value), while the October $340 gold call would have a premium of about $25 ($15 intrinsic, $10 time). Should gold rise $10 an ounce to $365, the August $340 call premium would probably go to about $26, an increase of $9, while the October call might climb only to $32, a jump of $7 (the other $3 of gold's price move would be absorbed by a change in the ratio of intrinsic value to time value).

In addition, the further an option is out of the money, the smaller the change in premium is likely to be in response to a change in the price of the underlying futures contract. In other words, a December $380 gold call would go up much less than a December $360 gold call on a move in the December gold futures price from $345 to $355, simply because the distance from the actual gold price to the $380 strike price is so much greater than the distance from the gold price to the $360 strike.

No limit on some option price moves

One other important point about premiums on some commodity futures options: exchange rules place a limit on the amount the price of a futures contract on many commodities can change in any one day (this is true of nearly all agricultural commodity futures). However, in many cases, there are no limits on the amount the price of a futures option can change (though, in some cases, trading in options is halted when the futures contract is "locked" in a limit-up or limit-down position).

Thus, on days when certain commodity futures are up limit or down limit, the premiums on options on those commodities may move much more than the futures prices, reflecting the true market value of the commodities rather than the limited futures values. (Among the options that fan into this category are those on sugar, cocoa, coffee, orange juice, lumber, live cattle, feeder cattle, live hogs, pork bellies, crude oil, heating oil, unleaded gasoline, natural gas, the CRB Index, the U.S. Dollar Index, and Eurodollars. Options with no limits, but trading lockouts, include those on the currencies, the metals, and most of the domestic and foreign stock indices.)

As veteran futures market participants should recognize, the lack of a daily limit can make options extremely valuable trading tools. They can be used to offset potentially disastrous futures positions that otherwise couldn't be closed out once prices were down limit, and they can be used to buy into a rally and make extra profits even after futures prices have already moved up limit.

HOW OPTIONS ARE TRADED

As pointed out earlier, options are bought and sold on the trading floor of the exchange authorized to trade in that particular option. Exchange-traded options have many advantages over the old person-to-person options:

■ The exchanges match up original buyers and sellers.

■ They maintain a continuous "secondary market," enabling option buyers and sellers to liquidate their positions even when the other party to the original transaction wishes to retain his position.

■ They establish standard strike prices and expiration dates for options, adding new strike prices and option months in an orderly and predict able fashion.

■ They ensure that all trades conform to the same set of rules and that prices are recorded quickly — and accurately.

Following is a list of the major exchanges on which futures options trade and the types of futures contracts on which each exchange is authorized to trade options. Each of these exchanges has brochures and other informational material outlining exact contract specifications, trading months, price guidelines, and margin requirements. Since many of these details change from time to time and from exchange to exchange, I have not attempted to include them all in this book. Contact the exchange directly if you are considering trading a specific option and need more information than is available here or from your broker.

CHICAGO BOARD OF TRADE (CBOT):

Corn — 5,000-bushel contract

Oats — 5,000 bushel contract

Soybeans — 5,000-bushel contract

Soybean meal — 100-ton contract

Soybean oil — 60,000-pound contract

Wheat — 5,000-bushel contract

DJIA Index — $10 time the Dow Jones Industrial Average

Major Market Index — $500 times the Major Market Index value

Municipal Bond Index — $1,000 times the Municipal
Bond Index value

U.S. Treasury bonds — $100,000 contract

Inflation-Indexed U.S. Treasury Bonds — $100,000 contract

2-Year U.S. Treasury notes — $200,000 contract

5-Year U.S. Treasury notes — $100,000 contract

10-Year U.S. Treasury notes — $100,000 contract

Silver — 1,000-ounce contract

CHICAGO MERCANTILE EXCHANGE (CME):

Live cattle — 40,000-pound contract

Feeder cattle — 50,000-pound contract

Lean hogs — 40,000-pound contract

Frozen pork bellies — 40,000-pound contract

Lumber — 80,000-board-feet contract

Australian dollar — 100,000 Australian dollars

British pound — 62,500 British pounds

Canadian dollar — 100,000 Canadian dollars

Euro — 125,000 Euros

German mark — 125,000 German marks

Japanese yen — 12,500,000 Japanese yen

Swiss franc — 125,000 Swiss francs

NASDAQ 100 Index — $100 times NASDAQ 100 Index value

Nikkei Stock Average — $5 times Nikkei (Tokyo) 225 Stock Index value

S&P 500 Stock Index — $500 times Standard & Poor's 500 Stock Index value

S&P MidCap 400 Index — $500 the S&P MidCap 400 Index value

Eurodollars — $1 million contract

U.S. Treasury bills — $1 million contract

COFFEE, SUGAR & COCOA EXCHANGE (CSCE):

Cocoa — 10-metric-ton contract

Coffee — 37,500-pound contract

Sugar (#11 World) — 112,000-pound contract

KANSAS CITY BOARD OF TRADE (KCBT):

Wheat — 5,000-bushel contract

Mini Value Line — $500 time Value Line Index value

MIDAMERICA COMMODITY EXCHANGE (MACE):

Corn — 1,000-bushel contract

Soybeans — 1,000-bushel contract

Wheat — 1,000-bushel contract

U.S. Treasury bonds — $50,000 contract

Gold — 33.2-troy-ounce contract

MINNEAPOLIS GRAIN EXCHANGE (MPLS):

Spring wheat 5,000-bushel contract

White wheat 5,000-bushel contract

NEW YORK MERCANTILE EXCHANGE, COMEX DIVISION:

Copper — 25,000-pound contract

Gold — 100-troy-ounce contract

Silver — 5,000-troy-ounce contract

NEW YORK COTTON EXCHANGE (CTN):

Cotton — 50,000-pound contract

Orange juice — 15,000-pound contract

US. Dollar Index — $1,000 times CTN U.S. Dollar Index value

NEW YORK FUTURES EXCHANGE (NYFE):

CRB Index — $500 times Commodity Research
Bureau Index value

New York Stock Exchange Composite Index — $500 times the
NYSE Composite index value

NEW YORK MERCANTILE EXCHANGE, NYMEX DIVISION:

Crude oil — 1,000-barrel contract

Heating oil 42,000 — gallon contract

Natural gas 10,000 — MMBtu contract

Unleaded gasoline — 42,000-gallon contract

These and other exchanges are considering introduction of options on other futures contracts. As a result, you shouldn't be surprised if you come across listings on the financial page for options not included on the above roster.

Strike prices and trading months

Each option trading on the above exchanges — both puts and calls — is offered with a number of different strike prices and a number of different expiration months. Unlike stock options, which are exactly the same (except for expiration months) from one exchange to the other, options on commodity futures vary significantly, depending on the exchange and formula used for setting expiration dates and strike prices.

Since strike prices range from a few cents to hundreds of dollars, depending on the price and size of the underlying commodity futures contract, it would be nearly impossible to list all the strike prices currently being traded for each individual futures option. However, there is one general rule for establishing strike prices that applies to nearly all options on futures:

Whenever trading begins on a new series of options — in other words, when an existing group of options expires and new ones with a far distant expiration date are added — five different strike prices are established. One of these five is always at the money — the same or nearly the same as the market price of the futures contract at the time. Two other strike prices are set at levels higher than the current futures price, creating in-the-money puts and out-of-the-money calls; and the other two are set at a level below the current futures price, creating in-the-money calls and out-of-the-money puts.

The gap between the strike prices depends on the price of the underlying commodity, ranging from as little as half a cent, in the case of sugar, to $40, in the case of gold (when the gold price is above $800 an ounce; gold strike price intervals are $5 when gold is below $400 an ounce, $10 an ounce when gold is between $400 and $600 and $20 when gold is between $600and $800 an ounce).

Likewise, the change in actual value of an options contract as the price of the underlying futures contract moves from one strike price to another varies widely with the size of the contract and the price of the commodity. For example, a one-cent change in the price of a sugar option would represent a total gain or loss on the full options contract of $1,120 (112,000 pounds x 1-cent per pound), while a $20 move in the price of a gold option would be worth $2,000 (100 ounces x $20 per ounce).

As futures prices change by certain amounts, the exchanges introduce options with higher or lower strike prices. In other words, new options are created on the same futures contract, thus giving investors the ability to tailor option strategies that always reflect the current market conditions.

Expiration months on futures options always match up with months in which actual futures contracts come due for delivery (except on those futures, such as the currencies and some stock indexes, which have serial options). However, there is not necessarily an option for every month with a futures contract delivery date. In addition,

options are not available on all futures contracts at any given time —
usually, only the nearest three or four futures contract delivery
months have associated options available, and only the nearest one or
two months have actively traded options. Following is a partial list of
trading months for some of the more popular options on futures:

OPTION	TRADING MONTHS
Corn	March, May, July, September, December, plus serial options
Wheat	March, May, July, September, December, plus serial options
Soybeans	January, March, May, July, August, September, November, plus serial options
Soybean Meal	January, March, May, July, August, September, October, December, plus serial options
Soybean Oil	January, March, May, July, August, September, October, December, plus serial options
Cotton	March, May, July, October, December
Sugar	March, May, July, October, plus serial options
Cocoa	March, May, July, September, December, plus serial options
Coffee	March, May, July, September, December, plus serial options
Orange Juice	January, March, May, July, September, November, plus serial options
Live Cattle	February, April, June, August, October, December, plus serial options

Lean Hogs   February, April, June, July, August, October, December, plus serial options

Pork Bellies   February, March, May, July, August

Gold   Every month

Silver   Every month

Copper   Every month

Lumber   January, March, May, July, September, November, plus serial options

Crude Oil   Every month

Heating Oil   Every month

Unleaded Gas   Every month

Currencies   Every month, with three options each for March, June, September, and December futures contracts

Euro   Every month, with three options each for March, June, September, and December futures contracts

U.S. $ Index   Every month, with three options each for March, June, September, and December futures contracts

T-Bonds   March, June, September, December, plus two serial options for each futures contract month

T-Notes   March, June, September, December plus two serial options for each futures contract month

T-Bills   March, June, September, December plus two serial options for each futures contract month

Eurodollars	Every month, with three options each for March, June, September, and December futures contracts
DJIA Index	March, June, September, December, plus two serial options for each futures contract month
S&P 500	Every month, with three options each for March, June, September, and December futures contracts
NASDAQ 100	Every month, with three options each for March, June, September, and December futures contracts
NYSE Index	Every month, with three options each for March, June, September, and December futures contracts

As mentioned once before, an individual option is identified by the name of the commodity, the futures contract delivery month (or option expiration month, in the case of serial options), the strike price, and the type (call or put). For example, an "October 62 cotton put" would be an option to sell an October cotton futures contract at a Price of 62 cents a pound (the option itself would actually expire on the first Friday in September). Likewise, a March 12-cent sugar call would be an option to buy a March sugar futures contract at a price of 12 cents a pound (here, the option would expire the second Friday of February).

You should now have a fairly comprehensive understanding of exactly what options on futures are and how they work, so let's go on to a discussion of the various investment strategies that employ these options.

STRATEGIES USING OPTIONS ON FUTURES

A PLAN FOR VIRTUALLY EVERY MARKET CONDITION

I've stressed the versatility of options throughout this book for one very simply reason: they really are versatile! No matter what the market condition — from raging rally to perilous plummet to deadly doldrums — there is an option strategy designed to give investors a chance to profit from it, whether the investor's goal is pure speculation, orderly capital growth, or increased income.

Having thus made options sound like the best thing since sliced bread, I am now compelled to add that trading in options on futures is not for everyone. In fact, it can safely be said that there is no one investment that's absolutely right for everyone. Even if an options strategy fits your goals, it may not be right for you since both buying and writing options requires a special risk orientation and a proper mental attitude. In other words, no matter how profitable an investment might eventually be, it's no good if you lay awake nights worrying about it.

Therefore, you should view this book not as a recommendation regarding what you should do, but rather an illustration of some of the things you can do. You must make your own decision about employing a given strategy at a particular time — or at any time at all, for that matter. And, that decision should be based on a careful comparison of potential risks versus potential rewards, as well as on how well the strategy fulfills your own financial goals. Before you employ any of the strategies outlined, make sure options not only suit your investment objectives, but fit your personal disposition as well.

The first strategies we'll look at are the most simple — designed primarily for the investor who wants to trade in options, but who may not want to take corresponding positions in the underlying futures contracts. These include buying both calls and puts, as well as writing both covered and uncovered options.

Later, we'll move on to techniques involving the simultaneous purchase or sale of more than one type of option -referred to as spread, or combination, strategies.

And, finally, we'll cover some of the more advanced strategies involving options in various combinations with positions in the underlying futures.

Obviously, there are more complex strategies that won't be covered, but you probably will never need those — at least not until you've become well-versed in the use of these fundamental techniques.

BASIC STRATEGIES USING OPTIONS ON FUTURES

The simplest, and potentially most rewarding, strategies involve the outright purchase of an option on a futures contract. The motives behind these basic maneuvers, however, can vary widely. In other words, the purchase of a futures option has attributes that can make it appealing to both the most speculative investor and the most conservative.

As I mentioned briefly in Chapter 1, the most significant advantage afforded the option buyer is leverage. Anyone who has ever bought a house has used the magic of leverage.

Assume you want to buy a house that costs $100,000. The owner, being a benevolent sort, asks only a 10 percent down payment. So, you put $10,000 down and you control the rights to that $ 100,000 house. Then, as they used to say in the old movies, time passes. The value of the house rises to $150,000. You decide to sell.

Had you paid $100,000 cash when you bought the house, you'd have made a $50,000 profit — or a 50 percent return on your investment. However, because you put down only $10,000 — and still made $50,000 in profits — you've increased the return on your original investment 500 percent. Now THAT'S leverage.

Leverage works the same way on stocks — which you can currently buy with only 50 percent down — but you get really incredible leverage with both futures and options on futures. Sometimes you can control a futures contract for as little as one percent of its total dollar value (even less if you're buying "deep" out-of-the-money options).

Assume it's May, sugar is selling for 10 cents a pound and you think the price is going up in the next couple of months. If you want to profit from this expected move, you have three choices:

1. You can buy 112,000 pounds in the cash market, paying 100 percent of the value — or $11,200 (112,000 pounds x 10 cents/pound). This is highly unlikely (unless you own a candy factory), since you'd have to take delivery, store the stuff, and then resell it after the price rises. However, we'll list it as an alternative just so you can see the leverage principle at work.

2. You can buy a futures contract calling for delivery of 112,000 pounds of sugar at 10 cents a pound in October. This would let you control the same amount of sugar as the first choice, but you'd only have to put up, say, $1,000 as a margin deposit (this depends on your broker, but we'll use $ 1,000 for ease of calculation).

3. You can buy an October 10-cent sugar call, paying a premium of one-half cent per pound. Again, you control the rights to a full 112,000 pounds of sugar, but you have to pay only for the option contract — in this case a total cost of $560 (112,000 pounds x 0.5 cent/pound).

Let's assume that you were right: the cash price of sugar rose to 13 cents a pound by late August, and you decided to sell at that point. How would you have fared?

With the first choice, actually buying the physical sugar, you paid out $11,200. Selling it now at 13 cents a pound, you bring in $14,560 — meaning you have a profit of $3,360 (for purposes of our examples, we'll ignore commissions and carrying costs). That represents a return of 30 percent. Not bad — but wait!

With the second choice, buying the futures contract, your profit is the same (in closing out your position, you theoretically take delivery of the sugar at 10 cents a pound and immediately sell at 13 cents a pound for a 3-cent-per-pound profit, or $3,360). However, since you only had to put up $1,000 to secure your position, your return increases to 336 percent! Quite an improvement, no?

With the third option, buying the call on the October futures contract, the profit picture is slightly different. The option you bought for one-half cent a pound would now probably be worth 3.2 cents a pound.★ Thus, if you sold it, you would bring in a total of $3,584. Subtract the $560 you paid for it originally (remember, this was an actual payment, not just a deposit), and your profit is $3,024. That's obviously not as good as the profit of $3,360 on the other two alternatives, but let's look at the return before we get critical. Since your original investment was only $560, the $3,024 profit represents a return of 540 percent!

And, that, my friends, is leverage. Using futures, you increased your return more than tenfold — and, using options on futures, you increased it by a whopping 18 times!

WHAT HAPPENS IF YOU'RE WRONG

It's also important not to overlook the second most important advantage options offer investors — the limited risk. Had you been wrong — say, instead of rising 3 cents a pound, sugar fell 3 cents a pound — you would have really taken a beating on both your physical sugar position and your sugar futures position.

★- *Values are estimated because the rise in sugar prices alters the ratio of intrinsic value to time value, and the passage of time reduces the time value at an increasing rate. However, since the call gives you the right to buy a sugar futures contract calling for delivery at 10 cents a pound, and sugar is selling at 13 cents, it would have 3 cents worth of intrinsic value and perhaps 0.2 cents of remaining time value.*

The physical sugar would have declined in value from $11,200 to $7,840, meaning you would have lost $3,360 — or 30 percent of your investment.

The futures contract would have declined in value by the same amount, so your loss on it would have been not just the $1,000 you put up originally, but the full $3,360 — a loss on your investment of 336 percent (remember, leverage works both ways).

The call, however, would have simply expired worthless. True, this would represent a loss of 100 percent of your original investment (you have to pay some price for your leverage, even with options) — but this was only $560, six times less than the actual loss with the other two alternatives.

PLOTTING THE POSSIBLE SCENARIOS

Still another advantage of buying options is that you can plot all the possible outcomes of your investment at the very start. Let's look at a sample "scenario analysis" showing the possible outcomes at expiration (intrinsic value only) for the call purchase described above:

Sugar Price	Call Price	Call Value	Less Cost	Profit (Loss)
7 cents	-0-	-0-	($560)	($560)
8 cents	-0-	-0-	($560)	($560)
9 cents	-0-	-0-	($560)	($560)
10 cents	-0-	-0-	($560)	($560)
11 cents	.01	$1,120	($560)	$560
12 cents	.02	$2,240	($560)	$1,680
13 cents	.03	$3,360	($560)	$2,800
14 cents	.04	$4,480	($560)	$3,920

These outcomes apply, of course, only if you hold the option right up until its expiration date, when there is nothing left but real value. Obviously, if you close your position early, the time value can affect the projected results.

Nevertheless, I find making this assessment of the risk/reward possibilities very helpful in deciding the best option positions to go into. A simple chart like the one below, which you can make copies of, will help you in making your projections.

Option Scenario Analysis Worksheet				
Futures Price	Option Price	Value of Option	Original Option Cost	Maximum Profit/Loss

Now let's outline the two basic option-buying strategies, one for bull market conditions, and the other for markets with a negative outlook.

Strategy number one: buying a call

ATTITUDE: Bullish (you think that the price of the underlying commodity and, consequently, the futures contract is going up).

MOTIVATION: To profit from the expected rise in price without putting up the capital needed to buy the actual commodity or accepting the risk of the actual futures contract.

RISK: Limited to the amount of premium. paid for the option.

PROFIT POTENTIAL: Unlimited; as long as the price of the futures contract continues to rise during the life of the option, the options value — and your profit — will continue to increase.

EXPLANATION OF STRATEGY. If the price of the commodity, and thus the value of the futures contract, goes up as much as you expect, you will make a profit. If you are wrong and the future stays at its current level or goes down, you could lose all or part of the premium paid for the option — but no more.

Before we go any further, I should point out that the buying of options, whether puts or calls, is considered speculation rather than investment. However, you should also realize that there is more than one degree of speculation. This is particularly true with options, where the strike price of the option you choose to buy drastically affects your prospects for success. Solely for that reason, I like to break option buyers down into three different groups according to just how speculative their purchases really are and, in so doing, explain the three sub-strategies available to call buyers.

I call my three groups of buyers Gamblers, Traders and Bankers. To illustrate, let's use an example using options on gold futures.* Assume that it's early September and the December gold futures contract is priced at $362 per troy ounce (meaning the cash price of gold is around $357 or $358 an ounce).

Each of our three potential option buyers thinks the price of gold, and thus the value of the futures contract, is going to rise to $400 in the coming months, and each has a total of $2,400 he's willing to commit to options. Let's see how each decides to spend his money.

With the December gold futures contract priced at $362, there would be three December calls worth considering. (Remember, by the way, that December refers to the futures contract delivery month, not necessarily the option expiration month. In this case, the options would expire the second Friday in November.)

(*NOTE: The Commodity Exchange, Inc., New York, NY, has given permission to adapt and reprint an excellent series of charts they prepared to portray graphically many of the strategies we'll be talking about. As a result, I will use the Comex gold and silver futures options in many of my examples of how the various strategies work. The prices quoted in both charts and examples were chosen primarily to illustrate the strategies and may not bear any relation to actual market prices at the time you read this.)

These would be:

- The December $340 in-the-money call.

- The December $360 at-the-money call.

- The December $380 out-of-the-money call.

(At the time this book was written, the odd-numbered strike prices at $10 intervals — i.e., $350, $370, etc. — were still fairly new and had not yet become popular, meaning liquidity was limited. For that reason, our examples will concentrate on the even-numbered strike prices at $20 intervals.)

The premiums on each of the three options would probably be somewhere in the vicinity of the following:

- $24 for the in-the-money $340 call ($22 intrinsic value and $2 time value), meaning each option contract would cost $2,400 (100 ounces x $24/ounce).

- $12 for the at-the-money $360 call ($2 intrinsic value and $10 time value), meaning each option contract would cost $1,200 (100 ounces x $12/ ounce).

- $3 for the out-of-the-money $380 call (zero intrinsic value and $3 time value), meaning each option contract would cost $300 (100 ounces x $3/ ounce).

Given these strike price levels and premiums, here's a projection of what each of our three types of buyers would probably do (along with a brief description of each):

The Gambler is out to make a killing. He's sure gold is going to rise sharply and wants to make the most of it. Usually, his only concern is making sure that, if he's wrong, he gets out with enough of a stake to try for the big killing one more time. Since he'll make more money the more gold he controls, he'll most likely opt for the out-of-the-money December $380 calls. With his $2,400 stake, he can buy eight of these options. All he's buying is time value of course, and gold would have to move up by $18 an ounce in only two months before his options gained any intrinsic value- but that doesn't bother him. He's more than willing to make an all-or-nothing play.

Take a look at the following table and you'll easily be able to see just why the Gambler's position is an all-or-nothing one. If he's wrong, and gold stays the same or moves down, he loses everything. If he's right and gold does move up, but only to $380, he still loses his entire $2,400. The Gambler must be is very right, to win as gold must go to at least $383 for him to break even. However, if he IS very right, the money really begins to roll in, earning him $800 in profit for every $1 dollar the gold futures contract moves above $383. And, if it hits his expected price of $400, he rakes in $13,600 in profits-a return of 567 percent! Here's how the whole thing looks (remember this is at expiration):

Gold Price	Call Price	Call Value	Less Cost	Profit (Loss)
$340	-0-	-0-	($2,400)	($2,400)
$360	-0-	-0-	($2,400)	($2,400)
$380	-0-	-0-	($2,400)	($2,400)
$383	$3	$2,400	($2,400)	-0-

$385	$5	$4,000	($2,400)	$1,600
$390	$10	$8,000	($2,400)	$5,600
$400	$20	$16,000	($2,400)	$13,600
$420	$40	$32,000	($2,400)	$29,600

Unfortunately, all too many newcomers to options slip into the Gambler category, succumbing to the lure of the low price and potential big profits of out-of-the-money options without realizing the huge increase in risk the cheapness and possible "Big Score" reflect.

The Trader is a different breed from the Gambler. He uses options intelligently as part of his overall commodity futures trading program, setting aside a certain portion of his funds for various options strategies, including hedging and an occasional foray into bolder speculation. He may position spreads or straddles to make money when a commodity price is moving slowly or showing no trend. Or, he may use options to lower the cost of a futures contract he wants to purchase or to lock in profits or reduce risk on one he already owns.

The key description of the Trader is that he is a person who knows all the things he can do with both options and futures to produce the kind of results he wants. Most successful participants in the commodity futures and options markets fall into the Trader category.

Our goal, here, is for you to become a successful Trader who knows what options can do and what you're doing when you use them.

As you can probably guess, the Trader demands a much better balance of risk and reward than the Gambler was willing to settle for. Given the same feelings about gold prices and the same set of option strike prices and premiums, the Trader would most likely take his $2,400 and buy two of the at-the-money December $400 gold calls. He's buying some real value-the $2 portion of the premium that reflects how far the call is already in the money — and a reasonable amount of time value given the remaining life of the option.

And, unlike the Gambler's options, if gold moves up, the Trader's calls should quickly follow, though probably not on a dollar-for-dollar basis. Once again, let's look at the table below to see how things could work out in November, when the calls expire:

Gold Price	Call Price	Call Value	Less Cost	Profit (Loss)
$340	-0-	-0-	($2,400)	($2,400)
$360	-0-	-0-	($2,400)	($2,400)
$372	$12	$2,400	($2,400)	-0-
$380	$20	$4,000	($2,400)	$1,600
$390	$30	$6,000	($2,400)	$3,600
$400	$40	$8,000	($2,400)	$5,600
$420	$60	$12,000	($2,400)	$9,600
$440	$80	$16,000	($2,400)	$13,600

See page 81 for how the profit/loss picture looks in graph form.

As you can see, the Trader doesn't have the chance to make nearly as big a killing as the Gambler — but his risk is much lower. If he's totally wrong and gold goes down, he loses his full investment just as the Gambler does. But if he's only a little wrong and gold stays around its price of $362 per ounce, he'll only lose part of his investment —in this case $2,000 of his $2,400. And, whereas gold had to move all the way to $383 before the Gambler broke even, the

Trader breaks even if gold goes to only $372, a move of just $10 instead of $21.

And, he's still got a shot at a fairly big score! If he's right and gold goes to $400 an ounce, he gets a 233 percent return on his investment — and that's certainly worth a moderate bit of speculation.

Now let's look at the Banker, the most conservative of the option buyers. Again, we take the same circumstances: the December gold contract is at $362 and the Banker thinks it's going to $400 within a few months (actually, the Banker is the type who would probably never figure anything was going to make that big a move that quickly, but let's ignore that), and he has $2,400 to work with.

GRAPH 1

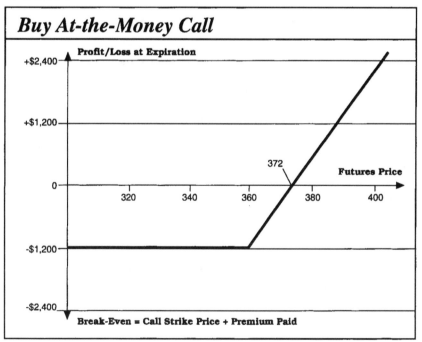

Graph Courtesy of The Commodity Exchange, Inc., New York, NY

He won't buy the December $380 calls at $3 because the risk is total-ly unreasonable. And, he probably won't even consider the December $360 calls because the risk factor is still too great and he'd have to buy too much time value. What he'll probably do if he real-ly wants to make a short-term play -and the Banker rarely takes a short-term position — is buy just one of the deep-in-the-money December $340 calls, priced at $24. That uses his entire $2,400, and offers the following possible results on the expiration date:

Gold Price	Call Price	Call Value	Less Cost	Profit (Loss)
$340	-0-	-0-	($2,400)	($2,400)
$360	$20	$2,000	($2,400)	($400)
$364	$24	$2,400	($2,400)	-0-
$370	$30	$3,000	($2,400)	$600
$380	$40	$4,000	($2,400)	$1,600
$390	$50	$5,000	($2,400)	$2,600
$400	$60	$6,000	($2,400)	$3,600
$420	$80	$8,000	($2,400)	$5,600

Once again you can see from the table that the Banker doesn't have the chance for as much profit as either the Gambler or the Trader. But, likewise, the risk factor is much, much lower. If the Banker is totally wrong and gold goes down, it has to drop all the way to $340 an ounce before he loses his fun investment. If he's only a little wrong and it stays around its current price of $362, he'll lose only a tiny por-tion of his funds — in this case, $200 of his $2,400.

If however, he's even a little bit right and gold goes up just $2 or $3, he'll break even or make a small profit. A move of just $8 an ounce, to $370, gives him a profit of $600 and a return of 25 percent, which is certainly enough to please most bankers. And, if he's totally right, and gold goes to $400 an ounce, he'll more than double his investment — not as good as the Gambler's 567 percent return or the Trader's 233 percent profit, but enough to make your typical banker absolutely delirious. And, he really didn't have that great a risk factor at all.

Thus, you can see that there are different ways to approach the buying of options — and while all of them have a little gambling flavor, some of them at least give you even-money chances — not just 20-to-1 odds.

TRADER FIRST – GAMBLER AND BANKER SECOND

Since we've already warned against the perils of being a Gambler and since the Banker buys options only sparingly, what you want to strive for is to become a knowledgeable and skilled Trader. Because The Trader usually opts for the balance of risk and reward offered by at-the-money options, we'll use those options to illustrate the rest of our strategies (though we win talk a bit more about the Banker when we get to option writing strategies).

Now that we've seen the basic strategy for our futures market bulls, let's move on to the most elementary technique employed by investors with a more bearish orientation — buying a put.

Strategy number two, buying a put

ATTITUDE: Bearish (you think the price of the underlying commodity and, consequently, the futures contract is going down).

MOTIVATION: To profit from the expected price drop without putting up the capital needed to sell the actual commodity short or accepting the risk of the actual futures contract.

RISK: Limited to the amount of premium paid for the option.

PROFIT POTENTIAL: Unlimited (except by a theoretical drop in the price of the commodity to zero); as long as the price of the futures contract continues to fall during the life of the option, the options value — and your profit — will continue to increase.

EXPLANATION OF STRATEGY: If the price of the commodity, and thus the value of the futures contract, falls as much as you expect, you will make a profit. If you are wrong and the future stays at its current level or goes up, you could lose all or part of the premium paid for the option — but no more.

Like buying calls, this strategy is best suited to the speculator. But, also like calls, there are different degrees of speculation, with each sub-strategy carrying a different risk factor. Since I've already covered the three basic sub-strategies in the discussion on buying calls, I won't repeat the discussion with regard to puts. We'll walk through one put-buying example with an at-the-money purchase — if you're unclear about the strategies for deep in-the-money puts or out-of-the-money puts, simply look back at the discussion on calls and reverse the numbers.

As with the calls, the at-the-money puts usually offer the most attractive combination of risk to reward — the combination favored by the experienced Trader in options on futures. This time, let's set up a hypothetical situation involving silver. It's late June and the COMEX September silver futures contract, representing 5,000 ounces of silver, is priced at $4.05 an ounce. Our Trader thinks silver is likely to drop in price over the next few months, perhaps enough to take the futures contract down to about $3.50 an ounce. He decides that purchasing September put options offers the best profit opportunity and has $2,000 to back his play.

The September $3.75 put, which is well out of the money, offers the biggest profit potential, but once again the risk is too high to suit the Trader. The September $4.25 put, though fairly far-in-the-money and thus carrying less risk, is also unacceptable because it doesn't offer a large enough potential reward.

The Trader thus turns to the at-the-money September $4.00 put, which has a premium of 20 cents, or $1,000 for the entire contract (5,000 ounces x 20 cents/ounce). With his $2,000, he buys two puts, thus setting up the following scenario at expiration:

Silver Price	Put Price	Value of Puts	Less Cost	Profit (Loss)
$4.50	-0-	-0-	($2,000)	($2,000)
$4.25	-0-	-0-	($2,000)	($2,000)
$4.00	-0-	-0-	($2,000)	($2,000)

$3.80	$0.20	$2,000	($2,000)	–0–
$3.75	$0.25	$2,500	($2,000)	$500
$3.50	$0.50	$5,000	($2,000)	$3,000
$3.25	$0.75	$7,500	($2,000)	$5,500
$3.00	$1.00	$10,000	($2,000)	$8,000

Here's how the scenario looks in graph form (profit/loss per put):

GRAPH 2

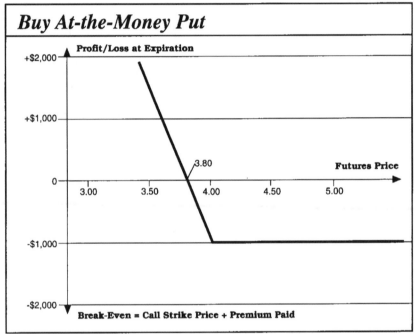

Graph Courtesy of The Commodity Exchange, Inc., New York, NY

Once again, the Trader didn't have nearly the chance to make a big killing like the Gambler could have by buying the out-of-the-money put, but his risk factor was also much lower. And, his return on the expected move in the silver futures contract price to $3.50 was much greater than the Banker could have earned with the deep in-the-money put. The Trader needs a downward move in the silver futures price of only 6 cents to give his put real value and a drop of only 25 cents to break even. After that, his profit multiplied quickly — and at his expected target price of $3.50, his return was a tidy 150 percent. Once again, a nice balance between risk and reward.

This is what determines the strategy you choose in buying options. The smaller the risk, the lower the possible reward — and the greater the risk, the larger the potential profit.

If you feel comfortable with the strong possibility of losing your entire investment, then you may want to play the Gambler's game and go for the big score. On the other hand, if the thought of losing every penny of your investment keeps you awake nights, you'd probably want to try the Banker's ploy.

But, for day-to-day consistency and balanced odds, the best choice is probably the path taken by the Trader — the at-the-money option.

Your personal goals must determine your strategy. Whether it's calls or puts, if you're going to be a straight buyer of options be sure you make yourself comfortable!

DECIDING TO GET OUT EARLY

The scenarios I've outlined carry the option position all the way to expiration. In real life, that's not necessary. Simply because you're wrong, you don't have to lose the entire premium you paid.

At any time before the option you bought expires, you can generally sell it and recover at least some of the original cost. Even if an option stays out of the money — meaning it has no intrinsic value —it's almost always possible to sell it for the remaining time value, even if only a few cents.

In fact, deciding to take either a profit or a loss before your option expires is one of the most difficult aspects of trading in options. Using the above example again, assume that the September silver futures contract had dropped to $3.90 by mid-July. Even though your break-even point at expiration is $3.80, you could, in fact, have a profit now with the remaining time value. When you bought your put, you paid 20 cents in time value. At this point it has 10 cents of real value and could retain perhaps 15 cents of time value. Thus, if you decided to sell it, you could probably get around 25 cents, netting a profit of $250 per contract — even though silver prices didn't fall nearly as much as you expected.

Likewise, if silver stayed the same (or even went up a bit), your put would retain enough time value so that you could get some of your original investment back.

There are really no firm guidelines for when to sell an option prior to expiration. The best method is to simply evaluate every position when you open it, setting both a profit goal and a loss limit — and sticking to them throughout the life of your option.

Don't get stubborn when you're wrong and refuse to take your loss - undue optimism about a coming turnaround can do nothing but compound your original error in judgment. Likewise, don't get greedy. Investors who try to ride a winning position too far lose more profits in the options market every day than most of us will make in a lifetime! If you want to be a successful Trader, set realistic goals and tolerable loss limits — and stick to them. You may miss a few big killings, but you'll save your neck and your money a lot more often!

WRITING OPTIONS ON FUTURES

Now that we've covered the basic option buying strategies, we'll take a look at the opposite side of the coin — selling, or writing, options on futures. Even though it should be obvious, many people overlook the fact that whenever someone buys an option, someone else must sell that option. Accepting that, then, the question becomes: "Why write an option?" After all, if the option buyer gets limited risk and unlimited profit potential, then the option writer must be accepting unlimited risk and limited profit opportunity. Why would anyone want a deal with those terms?

Actually, there are several reasons, but the basis for each is the premium the money the writer of the option receives from the buyer. In some cases, the premium may be viewed strictly as a return on investment, much like the interest payment on a bank account. In others, the premium from selling options is viewed as a way to increase the profit from a position in the underlying futures contract. And, in still others, the premium is considered a means to reduce the risk associated with a new futures position or to lock in profits on an established one. Finally, and perhaps most importantly, the writing of options is one of the few ways to generate profits — in the form of the premium — when the market is going neither up nor down with any conviction. Let's look at the basic option-writing strategies.

Strategy number three: writing a naked call

ATTITUDE: Neutral or slightly bearish (you think the price of the underlying commodity and, consequently, the futures contract will remain unchanged or decline slightly).

MOTIVATION: To profit from this lack of firm direction in the market.

RISK: Unlimited; if the price of the futures contract moves strongly upward during the life of the call you sell, the options value —and your losses — will continue to increase.

PROFIT POTENTIAL: Limited to the amount of premium received for the call you sell.

EXPLANATION OF STRATEGY: If the price of the commodity, and thus the value of the futures contract, stays near or below the striking price of the call you sell, you will make a profit. If you are wrong and the future moves strongly upward, you could lose just as much as would someone who sold the futures contract short, minus the amount of the premium you received.

You'll notice that I have named the calls "naked". This simply means that you do not own a corresponding position in the underlying futures contract. When you have a long position in the futures contract and write a call, this is referred to as a "covered" position, which will be discussed later.

As mentioned previously, writing naked calls (or covered calls, for that matter) is one of the few profitable strategies that can be employed during those all too frequent markets that are neither strongly bearish nor strongly bullish — that is, neutral or "flat" markets.

The most common goal behind writing naked calls is the generation of cash flow (from premiums received) during periods when the market is stable or declining slightly. A warning, however: even though it may seem extremely simple to pick out a flat market, the risks entailed are great. Writing naked calls (or puts, which we'll discuss later), should be considered only by those who fully understand the risks and who are emotionally willing and financially able to assume them.

Why this stern warning regarding risk? Because, if futures prices rise, then call prices will also rise — almost dollar for dollar once the calls get in the money. To guarantee that you will fulfill the terms of the option, you must put up a margin deposit any time you sell a call. Thus, if prices go against you to the extent that it would take more money to fulfill those terms, you may be subject to a "margin call" from your broker. When this happens you must either take your loss or put up more money. If you chose the latter course, then you can keep losing money as long as you refuse to close out the position. Thus, the potential loss, as mentioned before, is unlimited.

Let's use the same set of circumstances we used in our earlier silver example and see just how the scenario might look for a naked call writer. Again, assume it's late June and the COMEX September silver futures contract, representing 5,000 ounces of silver, is priced at $4.05 an ounce. This time, however, our typical Trader thinks the silver market is going to be relatively stable, with no big moves in either direction. Since, under those circumstances, no big profits could be generated by buying either calls or puts, the Trader decides to write naked calls. For ease of calculation, let's say he sells just one September $4.00 silver call, receiving a premium of 20 cents an ounce, or $1,000 total for the full option contract (5,000 ounces x 20 cents/ounce).

This time, the Trader doesn't care whether silver drops to $3.50 an ounce or not —just so long as it stays at or below $4.00 an ounce. Let's look at another scenario table to see what happens if it does —and if it doesn't. (Most option writers sell the puts or calls with the intent of having them expire worthless. Thus, carrying a scenario to expiration is much more valid for option writers than for option buyers.)

Futures Price	Call Price	Call Value	Premium Received	Profit (Loss)
$3.50	-0-	-0-	$1,000	$1,000
$3.75	-0-	-0-	$1,000	$1,000
$4.00	-0-	-0-	$1,000	$1,000
$4.05	$0.05	($250)	$1,000	$750
$4.20	$0.20	($1,000)	$1,000	-0-
$4.25	$0.25	($1,250)	$1,000	($250)
$4.50	$0.50	($2,500)	$1,000	($1,500)
$4.75	$0.75	($3,750)	$1,000	($2,750)

As you can see, the maximum possible profit for the call writer is $1,000 (less commissions) — the amount of premium received when the call was sold — no matter how low the price of the silver futures contract falls.

On the other hand, the call writer's loss can continue to climb as long as the price of the silver futures contract rises. However, the premium received provides some protection against a price rise — the writer will make money on his position at any futures prices below $4.20. This "cushion" is a result of the time value inherent in option premiums.

Only one thing is absolutely certain in option trading and that is that time price, the time value will erode. The graph below shows the typical pattern of time value erosion in options. Note how the rate of erosion increases the closer the option gets to expiration. This erosion is one of the key profit elements for a writer of options.

GRAPH 3

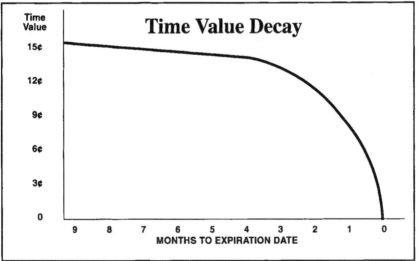

Graph Courtesy of The Commodity Exchange, Inc., New York, NY

Here's how the option-writing scenario looks in graph form:

GRAPH 4

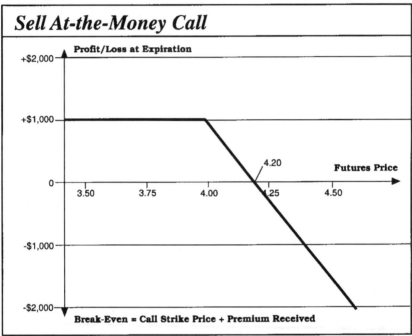

Graph Courtesy of The Commodity Exchange, Inc., New York, NY

At the risk of belaboring a point, I feel I should repeat that the writing of naked call options is appropriate only when prices are expected to be flat to lower — i.e, when there are few signs that the futures price will move above the option strike price. Even though a writer of naked calls wants those cans to expire worthless, he should be prepared to get out quickly of the option position by making an offsetting purchase should an unexpected rise in the futures price occur.

TWO OTHER KEY POINTS FOR OPTION WRITERS

Before we move on to a discussion of writing puts, there are two other key points that any writer of options must consider:

The first is that the right to exercise an option is solely the right of the option buyer.

The second is that the buyer of an option has the right to exercise that option at any time up to the date on which it expires.

In reality, very few options are ever exercised — most option buyers simply take their profits or losses by selling an option identical to the one they bought. One standard exception to this rule involves deep in-the-money options; those having substantial intrinsic value and little time value. If the time value approaches zero — or worse, disappears entirely — then the deep in-the-money option will almost certainly be exercised prior to expiration.

Thus, every writer of options should be aware of the possibility of exercise, which can result in his having to take a position in the underlying futures contract at the option strike price — sometimes at significant financial cost.

With that in mind, let's look at the writing of naked put options.

Strategy number four: writing a naked put

ATTITUDE: Neutral to slightly bullish (you think the price of the underlying commodity and, consequently, the futures contract will remain unchanged or rise slightly).

MOTIVATION: To profit from this lack of firm direction in the market.

RISK: Unlimited; if the price of the futures contract moves strongly downward during the life of the put you sell, the options value — and your losses — Will continue to increase.

PROFIT POTENTIAL: Limited to the amount of premium received for the put you sell.

EXPLANATION OF STRATEGY: If the price of the commodity, and thus the value of the futures contract, stays near or above the striking price of the put you sell, you will make a profit. If you are wrong and the future moves strongly downward, you could lose just as much as would someone who bought the futures contract, minus, the amount of the premium you received.

Just as you can write call options for premium income without taking a position in the underlying futures contract, so can you write put options. And, just as the writer of naked calls takes substantial risk for a reward limited to the option premium, so does the writer of naked puts.

Indeed, the only difference is that the put writer's risk comes if the futures price goes lower than the option strike price, rather than higher, as with calls.

Let's look at an example using gold. As in our call-buying situation, assume that it's early September and the December gold futures contract is priced at $362 per troy ounce (meaning the cash price of gold is around $357 or $358 an ounce).

Our Trader decides that the gold market is going nowhere fast, but feels that there's a slightly greater possibility it will rise rather than fall. Since he doesn't want to buy gold options on those terms, he decides to sell them and collect the premium. Because he's slightly bullish, though, writing calls is out.

Thus, he takes at look at the December $360 gold put, which is carrying a premium of $12, or $1,200 for the full option contract (100 ounces x $12/ ounce). Liking what he sees, he decides to write an option (again, this is for ease of calculation; most traders would do more than one contract in a situation like this).

Once again, take a look at the table below to see how his position could work out at expiration (remember, the December puts expire in November):

Futures Price	Call Price	Call Value	Premium Received	Profit (Loss)
$400	-0-	-0-	$1,200	$1,200
$380	-0-	-0-	$1,200	$1,200
$360	-0-	-0-	$1,200	$1,200
$348	$12	($1,200)	$1,200	-0-
$340	$20	($2,000)	$1,200	($800)
$320	$40	($4,000)	$1,200	($2,800)
$300	$60	($6,000)	$1,200	($4,800)

Again, here's how the profit/loss picture looks in graph form:

GRAPH 5

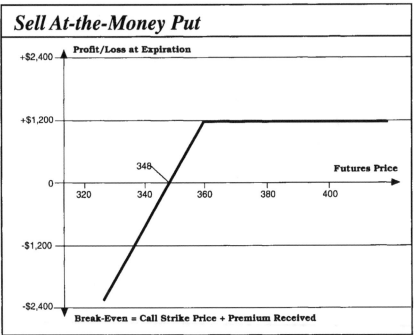

Graph Courtesy of The Commodity Exchange, Inc., New York, NY

As in the case of writing naked calls, the risk of writing uncovered puts is substantial. Thus, you should always be prepared to off set your position if prices unexpectedly begin to drop. All of the other warnings regarding call writing also apply to writing naked puts, so keep them firmly in mind when you consider this strategy.

SPREADS AND STRADDLES: PLAYING OPTION AGAINST OPTION

There are all kinds of ways to use options in combination with other options. Some offer the possibility of fantastic returns — and correspondingly high risk — and others suit the needs of the most conservative investor. Some offer fantastic leverage, requiring little or no cash up front, while others define absolutely the range in which you can expect profits and what those profits will be. In other words, you can combine options to achieve almost any goal.

I'm going to outline some common — and a couple of not so common — combination strategies. Since we've covered the four basic strategies involving individual options, my explanations of these techniques win not be as lengthy as some of the earlier ones. All I'll be doing is showing you how puts and calls go together to make up spreads and straddles.

Placing orders for combinations

First though, a few words about putting in your orders. Orders to buy and sell individual options are just like orders to buy and sell individual futures contracts. However, there are two different schools of thought on ordering option combinations. Many people advocate never placing what are called "combination orders." They say: "Buy the long side (the options you are going to own) at the price you want to pay. Then, once you've got those and are covered, sell the other side of the combination at the price you want on those."

This is called" legging in," and it may work most of the time. But I've found you can often also wind up owning one side of a carefully thought out combination and not be able to position the other side. This increases your risk factor considerably since you then become a simple option buyer. It also increases your cost factor — and, if you don't have enough cash to completely pay for the buy-side of your combination, you might have to sell the options back immediately, probably at a loss.

I recommend that you avoid legging into your combinations unless your broker's operation is a real disaster area when it comes to options. A good brokerage operation won't blink an eye on most combination orders. And, most of the time my orders go through (the other complaint proponents of "legging in" have is that it's much harder to get a combination order executed than it is to position the two sides separately). Occasionally my broker won't be able to put a combination together at the price I want and I'll miss out on a good thing. But, it doesn't happen often — and, when it does, it's usually because I'd already missed the market anyway. Thus, ask your broker how he prefers to have you enter your combination orders, and give it a try.

While we're on the subject, I should also note that you can also "leg out" of positions, selling one side and holding the other. Most of the time, in fact, this is the way I close out. It gives you a chance to make a profit on both sides of the combination, or to take advantage of the extra time on "calendar spreads." But, remember, if you close out the long side (sell the options you own) without closing out the short side, you're subject to a margin can because the short options are now naked. And, if you close the short side first and hold the long side, there's always the possibility the price trend of the futures contract could reverse, turning the small profit you might have had on the whole combination into a large loss on the individual option.

Other than what I outlined earlier, I won't tell you how to close out because you'll make your decisions differently in each case. But be aware of the possible dangers of closing incorrectly. And, if none of your combination orders go through, I suppose you can try changing your method of placing orders — but I'd be more likely to suggest you try changing brokers.

For now, let's just concentrate on learning how the various combination strategies work. I'll start with two bull market strategies — a simple bull spread, which can be done with both calls and puts, and a bull calendar spread, applicable only to call. Then, I'll follow with a couple of techniques for bearish trends - the simple bear spread with both calls and puts and the bear calendar spread, which can be done only with puts. Finally, I'll show how you can use combinations to make money in both stable markets and markets with lots of volatility but no firm direction.

Strategy number five: the vertical bull spread

ATTITUDE: Bullish (you think the price of the underlying commodity and, consequently, the futures contract will go up).

MOTIVATION: To profit from this rise in price with a lower outlay of cash and a more firmly defined level of risk.

RISK: In the case of calls, limited to the net amount of premium paid (the premium paid for the call you buy, less the premium you receive for the call you sell). In the case of puts, limited to the difference between the strike prices of the two puts less the amount of premium received.

PROFIT POTENTIAL: In the case of calls, limited to the difference between the strike prices of two calls less the amount of premium paid. In the case of puts, limited to the net amount of premium received.

EXPLANATION OF STRATEGY WITH CALLS: You buy a lower strike price call and sell a higher strike price call expiring in the same month, paying the difference between the two premiums. If the price of the commodity, and thus the value of the futures contract, rises above the striking price of the call you purchase by more than the amount of the net premium you paid, you will make a profit. Your maximum profit will come if the price of the futures contract rises above the striking price of the call you sell; after that, the loss on one call will exactly offset the gain on the other. If you are wrong and the future moves strongly downward, all you can lose is the net amount of the premium you paid.

EXPLANATION OF STRATEGY WITH PUTS: You buy a lower strike price put and sell a higher strike price put, collecting the difference between the two premiums. If the price of the commodity, and thus the value of the futures contract, rises above the striking price of the put you purchase by more than the amount of the net premium you received, you will make a profit. Your maximum profit will come if the price of the futures contract rises above the striking price of the put you sell; after that, both puts will expire worthless and you will keep the net premium received. If you are wrong and the future moves strongly downward, you lose the difference between the two strike prices, less the amount of the premium you received.

The Vertical Bull Spread is exactly what it sounds like. Vertical means "up and down" — and that's how futures prices move. Bull means you think the futures price is going up.

The theory is the same whether you choose to use calls or puts, but two factors influence which you want to use. The first, and most important, is the "spread" between the premiums on the options involved. The simplest way to do a Vertical Bull Spread is with calls since the call you sell is fully covered, meaning you have to put up no margin money. (The margin requirement is the second factor — with the Vertical Bull Put Spread, you must deposit the difference between the two strike prices, less the premium received to secure your position).

However, call premiums tend to be higher than put premiums and this sometimes distorts the spread, making puts more attractive. (Call premiums run higher because most market participants are optimistic unless the market is actually crashing; thus, they are willing to pay more to bet the market will go up than to bet it will go down. Option pricing theorists win deny the fact that calls carry higher premiums, telling you that, on a relative basis, call and put premiums are the same. That is certainly true in theory — and it may also be true in practice if you are dealing at the institutional level with large lots and tens of thousands of dollars. However, on small retail lots, where you are dealing with middlemen and hefty bid-ask spreads, the purchase price of calls will almost always be higher than puts on a relative basis and call spreads will generally be widen)

So, how do you determine whether the put spread or call spread is better? Let's look at a brief example. Assume that the August gold futures contract is priced at $315 and you expect it to rise to $330 before the August options expire. You want to do a Vertical Bull Spread involving the two options closest to the current futures price but don't know whether to use calls or puts. You pick up your Wall Street Journal and look at the prices for gold options.

The August $300 gold call (the in-the-money call) has a premium of $21 and the August $320 gold call (the out-of-the-money can) has a premium of $8.40. (Again, we'll ignore the $310 calls because of their newness and poorer liquidity.)

Thus, if you buy the $300 call at $2 1, or $2, 100 for the full option (100 ounces x $21 /ounce), and sell the $320 call at $8.40, or $840 for the fun option, your net cost for the spread is $1,260. The difference between the strike prices is $20, thus the maximum profit you can make is $2,000 ($20 x 100 ounces), minus the $1,260 net premium you paid -or $740 per spread. The maximum risk, should the gold futures contract drop below $300, is the $1,260 premium you paid.

The August $320 gold put (the in-the-money put) has a premium of $12 and the August $300 gold put (the out-of-the-money put) has a premium of $3.80.

Thus, if you buy the $300 put at $3.80, or $380 for the full option, and sell the $320 put for $12, or $1,200 for the full option, you receive the difference — or $820 for the full spread. Again, the difference between the strike prices is $20. The maximum profit you can make is $820 — the net premium you received — while your maximum risk is $1,180 ($2,000 minus the $820 you got up front).

As you can see, the best way to do your Vertical Bull Spread under these conditions is with puts — you get $80 more potential profit and $80 less risk on each spread you sell.

Had you expected a bigger move in gold prices, say to $350 an ounce, you might have compared the out-of-the-money Bull Call Spread and the in-the-money Bull Put Spread — in other words, spreads involving the $320 and $340 strike price options.

We already saw that the August $320 gold call had a premium of $8.40, and we find that the August $340 gold call has a premium of $3.40. If we buy the $320 call for $840 and sell the $340 call for $340, our net cost is $500. If we're wrong and the gold futures contract stays below $320 an ounce, the most we can lose here is $500. If we're right and gold goes above $340 an ounce, we can make $1,500 profit.

Now what about the puts. The August $320 gold put had a premium of $12 and we find that the August $340 gold put has a premium of $26. If we sell the $340 put and buy the $320 put, we receive $1,400 ($26 - $12 x 100 ounces). This time, if we're right and gold goes above $340, both options expire worthless and we keep the $1,400 as profit. if we're wrong and gold stays below $320, we lose $600.

Obviously, in this case, the calls would be the better choice for our Vertical Bull Spread, There's one item you should remember: the odds of being wrong on an out-of-the-money call spread or in-the-money put spread are much higher than on the first combination we discussed simply because the price of the futures contract has to move so much more — $5 an ounce in one case and $25 an ounce in the other. That's why the out-of-the-money $320-$340 call spread offers a $1,500 profit and a $500 maximum loss, while the $300-$320 call spread offers only $740 profit and a $1,260 maximum loss.

If you're wondering why anyone would use a spread instead of just buying an option outright, you need only add one more risk/reward comparison. In the example above, had an investor simply bought the $320 gold can instead of buying the spread, his possible profit would have been unlimited, but his cost — and thus his risk — would have been $840, instead of just $500. He accepted a limit on profit in order to cut his risk by $340. With puts, it's even more dramatic. Had an investor merely sold the $340 put instead of using the spread, his profit potential would have risen from $1,400 to $2,600, but his risk would have risen from $600 to an unlimited amount. He reduced his potential profit by $1,200 in order to put an absolute maximum on his risk.

The graphs, on the following pages show how the profit/loss picture looks on the Vertical Bull Call Spread and the Vertical Bull Put Spread, respectively.

The Buy Call Spread graph assumes an August gold futures price of about $400. An investor buys an August $400 gold call for a premium of $12 per ounce ($1,200) and sells an August $420 gold call for $7 per ounce ($700), a net debit on the premiums of $5 per ounce.

GRAPH 6

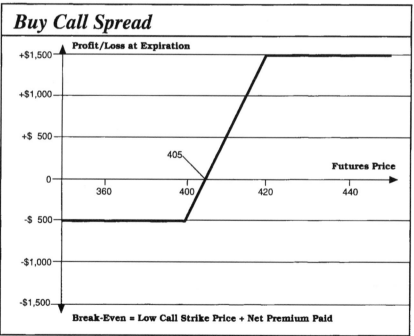

Buy Call Spread

Break-Even = Low Call Strike Price + Net Premium Paid

Graph Courtesy of The Commodity Exchange, Inc., New York, NY

As you can see, he loses everything if the futures price stays below $400, breaks even if it goes to $405 (the strike price of the call he bought plus the $5 premium he paid), and makes a maximum profit of $15 an ounce if it goes above $420.

THE PUT PICTURE LOOKS THE SAME

The Sell Put Spread graph assumes a September silver futures price of $4, with an investor selling a September $4.50 silver put for a premium of 58 cents an ounce, or $2,900 (58 cents/ounce x 5,000 ounces), and buying a September $4 silver put for a premium of 22 cents an ounce, or $ 1, 100. This time he gets a net credit on the premiums of 36 cents per ounce, or $1,800, on the full spread contract.

GRAPH 7

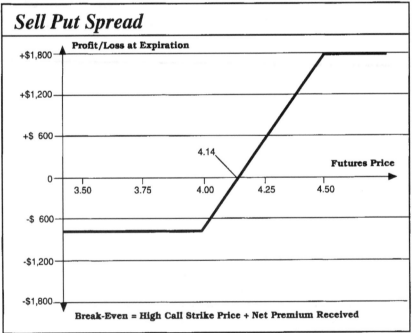

Sell Put Spread

Profit/Loss at Expiration

Break-Even = High Call Strike Price + Net Premium Received

Graph Courtesy of The Commodity Exchange, Inc., New York, NY

Again, he loses everything if the silver futures price stays below $4 an ounce, breaks even if it rises to $4.14 (the strike price of the call he sold minus the premium he received), and makes a maximum profit if the price of the silver futures contract goes above $4.50 an ounce, thus allowing both the put he bought and the put he sold to expire worthless.

Now, let's add the element of time to our bullish spread strategy with a look at the Calendar Call Spread.

Strategy number six: the calendar call spread

ATTITUDE: Bullish for the long term, but uncertain about when the upward move will start (you think the price of the underlying commodity and, consequently, the futures contract will go up, but think it could be a month or two before the move actually starts).

MOTIVATION: To establish a long-term option position without paying the higher long-term premium or accepting the risk that the upward move might not start before the cheaper short-term option expires.

RISK: Limited to the net amount of premium paid (the premium paid for the call you buy, less the premium you receive for the call you sell).

PROFIT POTENTIAL: Limited to the gain as a result of the faster erosion of time value on the short-term option until that option expires. Once the short-term option expires, however, the profit potential is unlimited.

EXPLANATION OF STRATEGY. You buy a long-term call and sell a short-term call with the same strike prices — i.e., buy an October $360 gold call and sell an August $360 gold call — paying the difference between the two premiums. If the price of the futures contract rises above the striking price of the calls before the short-term call expires, you will have to buy it back at a loss, which will be offset by the gain in the price of the long-term call you own. If the price of the futures contract stays below the striking price until after the short-term call expires, you then make a profit as soon as the futures price moves above the strike price by more than the amount of premium you paid. Your maximum profit is then unlimited. If the futures price falls, both calls will expire worthless and you will lose the premium you paid.

When we bought a call outright, the thing we wanted most was for the futures price to go up as fast as possible. With a Calendar Call Spread, we want the underlying future to go up — but not until we're ready.

I'll use gold again as an example. It's May, and the August gold futures price is $335. Because of the threat of higher inflation in the fall, we think gold — and thus the gold futures price — will go up, but we're not sure when. The August $340 gold call has a premium of $8.40, meaning we could buy an August option for $840 — but we're not certain gold will rise by July, when the August options expire, so we don't want to risk that much on a two-month play. And, we don't really want to pay the extra money for the October

$340 gold call, which has a premium of $15.20 ($1,520 for the full contract). As a result, we decide to try a Calendar Call Spread using options on both the August and October gold futures contracts. We buy the October $340 gold call for $1,520 and sell the August $340 gold call for $840. Our cost on the full Calendar Spread is thus only $680, less than we would have had to pay for the August call alone.

What we now want to happen is for the August gold futures price to stay below $340 an ounce until after the August calls expire in July. This would give us a profit of $840 on the calls we sold. Once that happens, we want the price of gold literally to soar — or at least rise enough so that the value of our October call exceeds the $680 we paid for the spread. Once that happens, we have a profit — and, if gold does soar, we have a huge profit.

Just to clarify how it works let's look at what could happen under several different sets of circumstances.

First, assume gold prices stay the same. This would mean that the August gold futures contract would be priced at about $335 and the August call we sold would expire worthless. If we still felt gold would rise, we could hold our October call just as explained above. If we no longer felt gold was going to rise, we could sell our October call, which should have a premium of about $8.40 (remember, that's what the August call had with two months of life left and gold prices at the same level). Thus, we would lose $680 on the call we bought ($1,520 - $840). But, remember, we made $840 on the call we sold since it expired worthless. Thus, we would make a profit of $160

($840 - $680) on our spread even though gold didn't move at all, simply because the short-term call lost time value faster than the longer term one.

Let's assume that gold went up sooner than we wanted, pushing the price of the August futures contract to $350 an ounce before the August options expired. At expiration, the August $340 call would be worth $ 10 per ounce, or $1,000. We would buy it back, taking a loss of $160 since we sold it for only $840. But remember, we now have a sizable profit on our October $340 call. The October futures contract would probably have a price of about $352, and our call, which still has two months of life left, would probably be worth about

---

(NOTE: *Even though both options in this example reflect gold prices, we're actually dealing with two different futures contracts. As a result, there may be some premium disparities between the options used in this strategy. In addition, some brokers may not consider the option you own on the October futures contract as a covering option for the option you are short on the August futures contract. Thus, you may encounter margin requirements with this strategy. As a result, this strategy is best suited for futures contracts that offer "serial" options — such as the S&P 500 and currencies. With these, you can buy and sell two different options calling for delivery of the same futures contract — e.g., both the February and March S&P 500 options call for delivery of the March S&P contract. You should also restrict your use of Calendar Spreads to the "hard" commodities, such as gold, silver, currencies, Treasury securities, and indices, rather than using them with "soft" commodities, such as grains, livestock, of foods. The reason is simple. There is very little difference between*

$26 an ounce, or $2,600. Thus, we have a paper profit of $1,080 ($2,600 $1,520), meaning our profit on the spread is $240 ($1,080 profit on long call minus $160 loss on short call minus $680 original premium paid). Again, this difference is explained by the loss of time value by the short-term call. Again, we have the choice of either selling our October call and taking our profit or holding it in hopes of more profit if gold goes still higher.

Finally, let's assume that gold prices did exactly what we wanted them to — stayed below $340 until late July, then went to, say, $370 by early September. The August $340 call we sold would have expired worthless, giving us a profit of $840. And, the October $340 call we bought would have gone to a little over $30 ($370 - $340, plus a little

---

100 ounces of gold delivered in July and 100 ounces of gold delivered in December, or between 125,000 German marks delivered in March and 125,000 German marks delivered in September. In fact, the very same gold or currency can be used over and over again to fulfill delivery requirements. That, however, is not the case with "soft" commodities. Forty thousand pounds of cattle delivered in June will be slaughtered, meaning another 40, 000 pounds will have to be found to fulfill a December delivery — and they could be substantially different in both price and quality due to shifting demand and other seasonal factors, such as the availability of feed. In other words, with most agricultural products and a few other commodities (such as oils) that experience severe seasonal price shifts, the mere fact that an option has a longer term doesn't make it suitable for covering a shorter-term option that calls for delivery of a different futures contract. Be careful in this area.)

remaining time value). If we sold out at $30, we'd get $3,000 for the option, giving us a profit on the call we bought of $1,480. Thus, we made a total profit on the spread of $2,320 — a return of more than 340 percent on our original $680 investment.

Had we ignored the spread strategy and just bought the August $340 call, we would have lost $840 since it expired worthless. Had we paid extra and bought just the October $340 call for $1,520, we would have still been able to sell it for $3,000, but our profit of $1,480 would have represented a return of only 97 percent.

Those figures alone should convince you of the merit of considering spread strategies rather than just blithely rushing out and buying an option when you think a commodity price is going up or down.

VARIATIONS ON RISK/REWARD PROJECTIONS

If you have a sharp pencil and like to play with numbers, you can calculate all sorts of variations on the basic bullish spread strategies I've outlined. You can sell more options than you buy —called "ratio writing" — and thus adjust your risk/reward ratios. You can buy more options than you sell and increase your potential profit. You can do Calendar Spreads with calls that are in the money, and thus have less of a debit due to the increase in intrinsic value and corresponding reduction in time value. Or, you can do lots of far out-of-the-money Calendar Spreads, etc.

If what I've told you about spreads so far is appealing, set down and work out your own variations and construct scenarios for them until you find one that exactly fits your needs. I'm sure it's there somewhere — after all, I've already told you just how versatile options can be.

One warning, however: don't get too enamored with the results your scenarios show. The key to profits with spreads is a widening of the difference between the price of the option you bought and the price of the one you sold — and that widening is almost always a function of changes in time value. Because the retention or loss of time value is so difficult to predict, it's extremely hard to get an exact advance picture of your potential reward, especially on in-the-money Calendar Spreads (that's why I haven't attempted to show a detailed scenario table or a graphic graph for the Calendar Spread — just too many variables). For your own calculations, though, you can generally figure that a spread that stays in the money will not widen much more than a point or so. Stick with this guideline and you should be able to construct reasonably accurate risk/reward projections on your spread strategies.

THE DIAGONAL SPREAD

Having said all of the above about figuring out your own spread variations, there is one favorite of mine I'd like to share — the Diagonal Spread.

It's a nifty little technique designed to give you a double play for your money — except it's not your money since these spreads should always be done for a net credit. What you're actually doing in a

Diagonal Spread is marrying the Vertical Bull Call Spread and the bullish Calendar Call Spread to create a mildly bearish combination. Here's how it works:

You sell a short-term call with a lower striking price and buy a longer-term call at the next higher striking price. A difference of more than one striking price is not recommended because of the hefty margin requirement; in fact, it's tough to make a Diagonal Spread work with options on high-priced commodities simply because the striking prices are so far apart.

You get the best part of the Calendar Spread — quick expiration on the calls you sell and more time for the calls you buy to get into the money. Primarily though, since you're using this as a bearish strategy, your motivation is to take advantage of a widening in the spread, not to get a big gain on your long cans after the short ones expire.

Since a lot of people think this is a pretty corny play, we'll use corn for our example. Assume it's late June; the 5,000 bushel September corn futures contract is priced at $2.54 and the December futures contract is priced at $2.57. You think corn may be going down, but you do not really want to sell a futures contract or buy a put. You look at the "Futures Options" column in The Wall Street Journal or Investor's Business Daily and find that the September $2.50 corn call is priced at 11.5 cents, or $575 for the full option contract (5,000 bushels x 11.5 cents/bushel). You then see that the December $2.60 corn call is priced at only 8 cents, or $400 per contract.

You decide to try a Diagonal Spread, selling the September $2.50 corn call at 11.5 cents and buying the December $2.60 corn call at 7 cents — a net credit of 4.5 cents, or $225 for the full Diagonal Spread. If September corn goes down as expected, the September $2.50 calls should expire worthless. You can then keep the $225 credit you received and sell the December calls, which should still be worth 3 or 4 cents, giving you a profit of between $375 and $425 on the spread. Or, you can hold them — with a guaranteed $225 profit — and hope corn rallies before your December calls expire, giving you a much better profit.

And, if September corn stays at its current level of $2.54 a bushel, the September $2.50 calls will lose all their time value and be worth only 4 cents a bushel. You can then buy them back for 4 cents, or $200, which still leaves you with a guaranteed $25 profit and, again, either sell or hold your December calls, for which you paid absolutely nothing.

Even if you were wrong, and September corn went up, you wouldn't lose much, if anything. Say it went to $2.65 a bushel, meaning the $2.50 call would be worth 15 cents a bushel. You'd have to buy it back, losing 4 cents a bushel, or $200, but your December $2.60 call would probably be worth 10 or 11 cents because of its time value. You could sell it at, say 10 cents, making 3 cents, or $150, profit and have a loss on the total spread of only $50 — even though you were totally wrong. Or, you could continue to hold it and hope corn continued to rise — after all, you still have three months before expiration.

A key point to remember here is to try to get the largest credit possible when positioning the spread —just don't go too deep in the money to get it. This increases your risk because the futures price has to decline more for the short calls to become worthless.

Diagonal spreads will also work with puts, but because of their lower time premium it's almost impossible to find good ones.

A general note on the subject of spreads and their prices: no matter what kind of spread you position, if it creates a debit, try to get the smallest debit possible. And, if it results in a credit, look for the largest credit possible. The key to continued success with spreads is to always sell more time value than you buy. If you do that, the spreads are almost bound to widen (or narrow, if it's that kind of strategy), providing you with at least a small profit no matter what the underlying futures price does or doesn't do.

Now that you've had this offbeat introduction to a mildly bearish spread strategy, let's move on to some of the more conventional spreads designed specifically for downward markets.

Strategy number seven: the vertical bear spread

ATTITUDE: Bearish (you think the price of the underlying commodity and, consequently, the futures contract will go down).

MOTIVATION: To profit from this drop in price with a lower outlay of cash and a more firmly defined level of risk than you could achieve by either shorting the futures contract or buying puts outright.

RISK: In the case of puts, limited to the net amount of premium paid (the premium paid for the put you buy, less the premium you receive for the put you sell). In the case of calls, limited to the difference between the strike prices of the two calls less the amount of premium received.

PROFIT POTENTIAL: In the case of puts, limited to the difference between the strike prices of two puts less the amount of premium paid. In the case of calls, limited to the net premium received.

EXPLANATION OF STRATEGY WITH PUTS: You buy a higher strike price put and sell a lower strike price put expiring in the same month, paying the difference between the two premiums. If the price of the commodity, and thus the value of the futures contract, falls below the striking price of the put you buy by more than the amount of the net premium you paid, you will make a profit. Your maximum profit will come if the price of the futures contract falls below the striking price of the put you sell; after that, the loss on one put will exactly offset the gain on the other (at expiration). If you are wrong and the future moves strongly upward, all you can lose is the net amount of the premium you paid.

EXPLANATION OF STRATEGY WITH CALLS: You buy a higher strike price call and sell a lower strike price call, collecting the difference between the two premiums. If the price of the commodity, and thus the value of the futures contract, falls below the striking price of the call you purchase by more than the amount of the net premium you received, you will make a profit. Your maximum profit will come if the price of the futures contract falls below the striking price of the call you sell; after that, both calls will expire worthless and you will keep the net premium received. If you are wrong and the future moves strongly upward, you lose the difference between the two strike prices, less the premium received.

The Vertical Bear Spread works exactly like the Vertical Bun Spread, except in reverse. Again, it makes no difference whether you use calls or puts unless you wish to avoid having a margin requirement (doing a Vertical Bear Spread with calls requires a margin deposit, since you are selling the call deeper in -or closer to — the Money). What you want to look at is the "spread" between the premiums. If you can get a better spread with puts, then that's the best way to do your Vertical Bear Spread, since the put you sell is once again fully covered (requires no margin deposit). The choice between using calls or puts for Vertical Bear plays is usually less distinct than for Vertical Bull spreads, again because calls carry a higher premium.

We'll use an example involving the same situation we had with the Vertical Bull Spread to demonstrate this play, so you'll be able to see the difference the higher call premiums make.

Again, we'll assume that the August gold futures contract is priced at $315, but now you expect it to fall to $290 before the August options expire. You want to do a Vertical Bear Spread involving the two options closest to the current futures price, but don't know whether to use calls or puts. You check your journal again and see these prices for gold options.

The August $300 gold call (the in-the-money call) has a premium of $21 and the August $320 gold call (the out-of-the-money call) has a premium of $8.40.

Thus, if you sell the $300 call at $21, or $2,100, and buy the $320 can at $8.40, or $840, your net credit (remember, last time we had a net debit on the calls because it was reversed) on the spread is $1,260. The maximum profit you can make should the gold futures contract drop below $300 an ounce is the $1,260 you just received, while the maximum loss you can take if it goes above $320 is $740 (the $2,000 difference between the strike price values, minus the credit you received).

The August $320 gold put (the in-the-money put) has a premium of $12 and the August $300 gold put (the out-of-the-money put) has a premium of $3.80.

Thus, if you buy the $320 put at $12, or $1,200, and sell the $300 put for $3.80, or $380 for the full option, you pay a net debit of $820 for the full spread (last time, we got a credit with the puts). With puts, the maximum profit you can make on the Vertical Bear Spread if gold goes below $300 an ounce is $1,180 (the $2,000 strike price difference minus the $820 you paid up front). Likewise, the maximum loss if gold goes above $320 is the $820 in premiums you paid at the start.

This time, even though the prices are exactly the same as in our previous example, the best way to do your Vertical Bear Spread is with calls, not puts -you get $80 more potential profit and $80 less risk on each spread you sell.

Again, had you expected a bigger drop in gold prices, say to $270 an ounce, you could have tried the in-the-money Bear Put Spread and the out-of-the-money Bear Call Spread — in other words, spreads involving the $280 and $300 strike price options. Again, though, the odds of being wrong would have been much higher, because of the larger price movement required in the underlying futures contract.

The Buy Put Spread and Sell Call Spread graphs show how the profit/ loss picture looks on the Vertical B ear Put Spread, and the Vertical B ear Call Spread respectively. As you study them, look back at Graphs 6 and 7 —you should note that the Vertical Bull Spread using calls is the virtual mirror image of the Vertical Bear Spread using puts and the Bear Call Spread mirrors the Bull Put Spread.

GRAPH 8

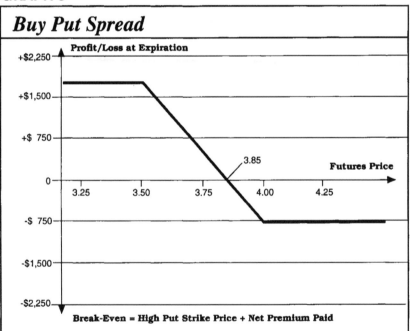

Graph Courtesy of The Commodity Exchange, Inc., New York, NY

Graph 8 assumes a September silver futures price of $4, with an investor buying a September $4 silver put for a premium of 30 cents an ounce, or $1,500, and selling a September $3.50 silver put for a premium of 15 cents an ounce, or $750, a net debit of 15 cents an ounce, or $750, on the fun spread contract.

Again, the investor loses everything if the futures price stays at or above $4 an ounce, breaks even if it falls to $3.85 (the strike price of the put he bought minus the 15-cent premium he paid), and makes his maximum profit of $1,750 if silver falls below $3.50.

GRAPH 9

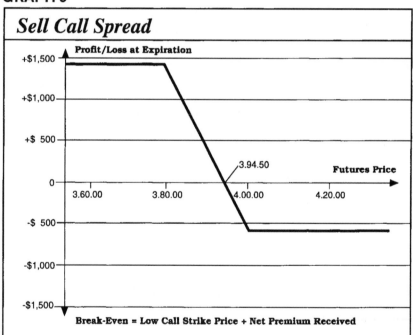

Graph Courtesy of The Commodity Exchange, Inc., New York, NY

Graph 9 assumes an August gold futures price of about $400. Our bearish investor sells an August $380 gold call for $26.50, or $2,650, and buys an August $400 gold call for $12 per ounce ($1,200), giving him a net credit on the spread of $14.50 an ounce, or $1,450.

Again, he loses everything if the gold futures price stays at or above $400 an ounce, breaks even if it falls to $394.50 (the strike price of the call he sold plus the premium he received), and makes a maximum profit if the price of August gold futures falls below $380 an ounce, where both calls would expire worthless.

Now, we'll repeat our previous process and add the element of time to our basic bearish strategy.

Strategy number eight: the calendar put spread

ATTITUDE: Bearish for the long term, but uncertain about when the downward move will start (you think the price of the underlying commodity and, consequently, the futures contract will fall, but think it could be a month or two before the move actually starts).

MOTIVATION: To establish a long-term option position without paying the higher long-term premium or accepting the risk that the upward move might not start before the cheaper short-term option expires.

RISK: Limited to the net amount of premium paid (the premium paid for the put you buy, less the premium you receive for the put you sell).

PROFIT POTENTIAL: Limited to the gain as a result of the faster erosion of time value on the short-term option until that option expires. Once the short-term option expires, however, the profit potential is unlimited.

EXPLANATION OF STRATEGY. You buy a long-term put and sell a short-term put with the same strike prices — i.e., buy an October $360 gold put and sell an August $360 gold put — paying the difference between the two premiums. If the price of the futures contract falls below the striking price of the puts before the short-term put expires, you will have to buy it back at a loss, which will be offset by the gain in the price of the long-term put you own. If the price of the futures contract stays above the striking price until after the short-term put expires, you then make a profit as soon as the futures price falls below the strike price by more than the amount of premium you paid. Your maximum profit is then unlimited. If the futures price rises, both puts will expire worthless and you will lose the premium you paid.

Since absolutely everything except the direction we want the price of the futures contract to move is the same with Calendar Put Spread as it was with the Calendar Call Spread, we won't go through another example. If you don't understand fully, just refer back to that section and reverse the entire scenario laid out there.

STRADDLE STRATEGIES

Now that we've seen several ways to make money with combinations when we think the market is definitely going up — or definitely going down — it's time to look at a pair of strategies for use when we're sure a futures market is going nowhere slowly — or everywhere in a big hurry. They're called straddles.

Strategy number nine: selling a straddle

ATTITUDE: Stable for the near term (you think the price of the underlying commodity and, consequently, the futures contract will stay relatively close to where it currently is with no strong trend either upward or downward).

MOTIVATION: To generate income on your capital during this period of trendless market action.

RISK: Unlimited. If the price of the underlying futures contract moves outside the range you've established, you can continue to lose money as long as the futures price continues to move in the direction of the breakout.

PROFIT POTENTIAL: Limited to the amount of premium received.

EXPLANATION OF STRATEGY. You sell an at-the-money call and also sell an at-the-money put with the same strike prices — i.e., sell an October $360 gold call and also sell an October $360 gold put —collecting both premiums.

The total of the premiums received establishes a "profit zone" and, as long as the price of the October gold futures contract remains within that zone, you make a profit. If the price moves outside that zone, however — either to the upside or the downside — you will lose the difference between the value of the in-the-money option you sold and the premium you received.

A straddle is simply a call and a put of the same term on the same futures contract, both bought or sold by the same person. A conventional straddle has the same striking price for both the call and the put, but straddles can also be modified and written with different striking prices.

The writer of a straddle usually positions it in anticipation of a stable market in the underlying commodity futures contract. The total of the two premiums collected when he sells it defines his break-even points, regardless of whether the futures price moves up or down, and also defines his maximum profit. He receives a less than maximum profit at any price inside the two break-even points. (The buyer of the straddle purchases it in anticipation of a volatile commodity price, and the premiums paid also determine his break-even levels, but for the buyer, the futures price must move outside those points.)

Let's see just how it works. It's early July and the October gold futures contract is priced at $401 an ounce. We think the gold market is going to stay reasonably stable over the coming few months, but we have a goodly amount of capital and would like to earn some income on it in the metals markets. Since buying neither calls nor puts will meet our needs and since writing either a call or a put exposes us to the risk of picking a direction for the market, we have just one choice: we decide to write a straddle. Checking quotes, we find that the October $400 gold call is selling for $14 and the October $400 gold put is priced at $10 (again, calls usually carry more premium).

We put up our capital (somewhere in the range of $4,000, depending on the broker) and write an October $400 gold straddle, collecting a total premium of $24 an ounce, or $2,400 on the full position. *(NOTE: A straddle writer does not have to sell the two options together as a straddle — he can sell them individually to two different buyers. The result is the same. Likewise, a straddle buyer can buy the two individual options that make up the straddle from different sellers.)*

Once we know the amount of premium we received, we can exactly define our potential profit and our break-even points. In this case, our maximum profit is $2,400 if the October gold futures contract is priced at exactly $400 an ounce when the options expire (they'll both be worthless and we keep the full premium). Our break-even point to the upside is $424 — the strike price plus the premium we received — and our break-even point to the downside is $376 — the strike price minus the premium received.

If the October gold futures contract is at $390 when the options expire, the call expires worthless and we buy back the put for $10, making a $14 an ounce profit. If the October gold futures contract is at $420 when the options expire, the put expires worthless and we buy back the call for $20, making a $4 an ounce profit. Once the gold futures price goes either above $424 or below $376, however, we begin losing money. For example, if the futures contract is at $360, the $400 call expires worthless but we have to buy the put back at $40 an ounce, losing $16 an ounce, or $1,600 on the full straddle.

Graph 10 shows exactly how the straddle works.

GRAPH 10

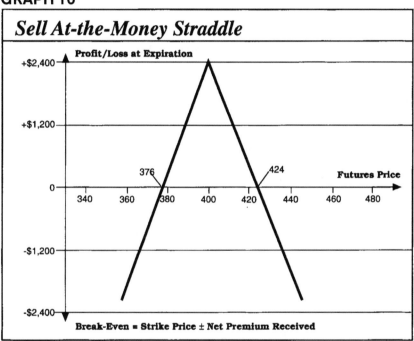

Graph Courtesy of The Commodity Exchange, Inc., New York, NY

As you see, our profit picture looks like a pyramid. The only unknown is the amount of loss, which increases $100 with every $1 move in the futures price either above or below the break-even levels of $376 and $424. (Invert the whole thing and you get the straddle buyer's profit picture, which you'll see when we discuss buying straddles in the next few pages.)

Straddle writing is obviously an ideal income strategy in a stagnant market. And, as with spreads, the straddle writer obviously wants to collect the largest premium possible to give himself the maximum possible profit and the widest possible range between his break-even points (the wider the range, the greater his protection against loss).

Obviously, everything we've said so far is based on carrying the straddle to the expiration date for the options. In reality, you'll find that very few straddles last until the expiration date. The writer will try to close out the short put at a profit on the first significant cyclical upswing and then buy back the short can at a profit when the zig-zagging market runs back down (the buyer tries to do the same thing, only he closes out his long call on the upswing and buys back his long put on the downward move).

THE MODIFIED STRADDLE STRATEGY

A modified straddle strategy works the same way as a conventional straddle, but instead of looking like a pyramid, the profit/loss picture is more like a plateau. The writer sells a put and call on the same futures contract, but the options have different strike prices. In the case of the October gold futures outlined above, a writer of a modified straddle would probably sell the October $420 gold call for a premium of about $6 and the $400 gold put, again for $10.

His maximum profit is again the total amount of premium received —in this case, $16 an ounce, or $1,600 on the full position. This offers obviously a smaller potential profit than a conventional straddle. In exchange for accepting less profit, however, the trader gets to keep the entire amount at any gold futures price level between $400 and $420 an ounce. His break even points also move to $384 on the downside and $436 on the upside — a range of $52 instead of only $48 with the conventional straddle.

The problem with the modified straddle is that you have to adopt either a mildly bullish or mildly bearish stance, which you may not feel comfortable doing. In the example above, the writer of the modified straddle had to decide that gold was more likely to move up somewhat than it was to move down, otherwise he would not have been willing to move his downside break-even point from $376 up to $384. Had he felt that gold was more likely to move down somewhat, rather than up, he probably would have written a modified straddle using the $400 gold call and the $380 gold put. This would have probably also earned him a total premium of about $1,600, but his upside break even point would have dropped to $416 and his downside level would have gone to $364.

The buyer of a modified straddle again has exactly the reverse profit/loss picture from that of the writer. Buying modified straddles is not generally recommended because there is a much wider range of futures prices at which the buyer loses his entire investment — in our example above, a buyer would lose everything at any gold futures price between $400 and $420 an ounce. This is a substantial risk to take.

Remember, however, that this is not the type of position to buy and hold until expiration — which is why some people buy modified straddles. They are looking for wide price swings that will let them close out both sides at a profit during the life of the options. They never buy a modified straddle as simply a "set-it-and-forget-it" strategy.

To get a clearer picture of the straddle buyer's frame of mind, let's move on to this strategy.

Strategy number ten: buying a straddle

ATTITUDE: Extremely volatile (you think the price of the underlying commodity and, consequently, the futures contract will gyrate wildly up and down during the life of the options, or will break out and establish a strong upward or downward trend).

MOTIVATION: To profit from this price movement, no matter which direction it is in.

RISK: Limited to the amount of premium paid.

PROFIT POTENTIAL: Unlimited. If the price of the underlying futures contract moves outside the range you've established when you paid your premiums, your profits continue to increase as long as the futures price continues to move in the direction of the breakout.

EXPLANATION OF STRATEGY: You buy an at-the-money call and also buy an at-the-money put with the same strike prices — i.e., buy a December $360 gold call and also buy a December $360 gold put —paying both premiums. The total of the premiums paid establishes two "profit zones," one above the strike price by any amount more than the total premium you paid and the other below the strike price by any amount more than the total premium you paid. If the futures price stays anywhere inside the range between those two profit zones, however, you will lose the difference between the value of the in-the-money option you bought and the premium you paid.

The straddle buyer's profit/loss scenario is exactly the opposite of the straddle seller's situation. As such, the worst-case situation for the buyer would be for both options to expire worthless, meaning that the futures price exactly matched the striking price on the expiration date. Obviously, this is highly improbable, so it's rare that a straddle buyer will ever lose all his money. And, the farther the futures price moves away from the striking price — in either direction — the less the straddle buyer will lose; or, once the break-even points are passed, the more the straddle buyer will profit.

The buyer of a straddle usually does so in anticipation of a highly volatile market in the underlying commodity futures contract. His best result would be to have the futures price move dramatically in one direction so he could sell one option at a profit, then move even more dramatically in the other direction, allowing him to also profit on his other option.

Let's see just how it works. It's early July and the October gold futures contract is priced at $401 an ounce. We think the gold market is going to be extremely volatile over the coming few months but we don't know which way prices are going first. Since we can't commit to a direction, buying either calls or puts would be a bad move, as would positioning either bullish or bearish spreads. So, we buy a straddle, paying $14 for an October $400 gold call and $10 for an October $400 gold put — a total premium of $24, or $2,400 for our full straddle. (Again, you should remember that you don't have to buy both sides of your straddle from the same seller —just buy both the put and call separately).

Since we paid $2,400 for the straddle, we know that is our maximum loss should the gold futures price be exactly $400 when the options expire. We also have defined our break-even points — in this case, $424 to the upside and $376 to the downside. Any price higher or

GRAPH 11

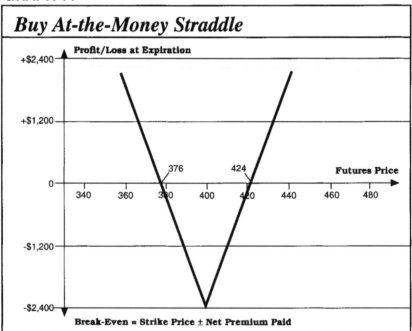

Graph Courtesy of The Commodity Exchange, Inc., New York, NY

lower than those two points and we make a profit at expiration. The size of the profit is limited only by the size of the futures price move. Graph 11 shows us how the situation looks graphically.

Now our profit picture looks like an inverted pyramid. The only unknown is the amount of profit, which increases $100 with every $1 move in the futures price either above or below the break even levels of $376 and $424. That's really all there is to it.

COMBINING OPTIONS WITH ACTUAL FUTURES CONTRACTS

As I've shown so far, the variety of potentially profitable options trading strategies which can be pursued without having a position — either long or short — in the futures market is almost endless. However, there are also a number of extremely rewarding plays that can be made by investors who understand how options can be bought or written in combination with futures positions. We will now touch on just a few of the most basic of these strategies involving both options and futures contracts.

The first strategies we'll discuss involve "covered" puts or "covered" calls. For those of you familiar with stock options, however, I should point out that there are some key differences between covered options on stocks and covered options on futures. In the first place, when stock owners think of covered option strategies, they generally think in terms of the stock they own covering options they want to sell.

Futures traders, on the other hand, generally think of the options they buy covering the futures contracts they either own or are short.

Another difference is that, barring bankruptcy or merger, a stock is a permanent asset. You can own it and write options on it over and over again. Futures contracts are different — like options, they have a specified life span after which they cease to exist. Thus, when you buy or write a covered option on a futures contract, you are in essence using a wasting asset keyed to the price of another wasting asset (at least it's wasting in the time sense, if not in price). With a stock, say IBM for example, you could write a July call, then an October call, then a January call, and so on — as long as IBM stock exists. With futures options, however, you have much less flexibility. A covered futures option is almost always keyed to the delivery month of the associated futures contract — i.e., if you're long a December futures contract, you usually don't fool around with October calls or puts, sticking instead to the December options.

As a result, covered option strategies with futures are not "income strategies," as they are generally considered to be with stocks. They are more accurately described as "insurance policies" designed to limit possible losses when going into a new futures position — either on the long side or the short side — or as devices to "lock in" profits on already established futures positions.

With that in mind, let's take a look at our first two covered option strategies, one designed for bull markets and the other for bearish trends.

Strategy number eleven: covered put purchase

ATTITUDE: Extremely bullish.

MOTIVATION: To profit from the expected upward futures price movement while establishing an absolute level of risk.

RISK: Limited to the loss of time value on the option, plus the amount — if any — that the put is out of the money.

PROFIT POTENTIAL: Unlimited. As long as the price of your futures contract continues to move up your profits will increase, minus only the amount of premium you paid for the protective put.

EXPLANATION OF STRATEGY: You buy a futures contract and also buy an at-the-money put for the same contract month — i.e., buy a December gold futures contract at $360 an ounce and also buy a December $360 gold put. The effect, if you are right, is the same as buying an at-the-money call — if the futures contract moves up in price, you profit fully, minus the premium you paid. If you are wrong and the futures contract moves down, you lose only the time value portion of the premium because the gain in intrinsic value in the put exactly offsets the loss on the long futures contract.

Since the risk/reward picture for this strategy is virtually the same as if you simply bought a call (at least at expiration of the option), you may wonder why anyone would bother. The chief reason is flexibility — with a can, you have only one chance for profit, but with a covered futures contract you may be able to gain on both sides of your position without losing your risk protection. This is possible because you have the option of "legging out" of either side of the position as market conditions change.

For example, assume that you bought the December gold futures contract at $360 in anticipation of a price rise and also bought the December $360 gold put for a premium of $10. If, on what you felt was only a temporary basis, the price of the gold futures contract dipped to $350, you could sell the put at a profit of perhaps $5 or $6 an ounce. The profit would give you some cushion against a further decline in the futures price and, if the futures price went back up as you anticipated, you could then sell it at a profit as well. Likewise, if the futures price rose and you decided to take a profit on the contract, you could continue to hold the put in anticipation of a pullback before expiration.

For the conservative investor this strategy is also much better than the solo purchase of the futures contract because the put provides "insurance" against the possibility of an unexpected decline in the futures price, strictly limiting the risk normally associated with any long futures position. Using the same example (the $360 gold position), your maximum loss would be $1,000, occurring at any futures price below $360 at expiration. Your break-even point would be $370 and your profit would be unlimited. The "premium" on this "insurance policy" would be any portion of the $ 10 put premium that you lost due to either the passage of time or a rise in the futures price.

Graph 12 shows how the Covered Put Purchase profit/loss picture appears in graph form. It assumes purchase of a silver futures contract at $4.00 and purchase of a $4.00 silver put at a premium of 20 cents an ounce, or $1,000 for the full contract. As you can see, the maximum loss at expiration is $ 1,000 at any futures price below $4.00, the break even point is $4.20 (futures purchase price plus option premium paid), and the profit potential is unlimited.

GRAPH 12

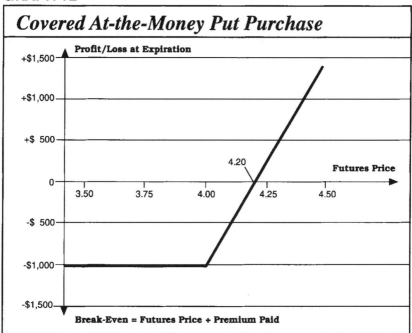

Covered At-the-Money Put Purchase

Graph Courtesy of The Commodity Exchange, Inc., New York, NY

Though we recommend the use of at-the-money puts in this strategy, it is possible to do it with other puts as well — it all depends on the amount of risk you are willing to accept on the futures contract. In the example used earlier, you could also buy a $340 gold put for, say $4. This would provide less protection since the put would not begin offsetting losses on the futures contract until the futures price dropped below $340, but it would also lower the break even point. The maximum loss here would be $2,400 ($2,000 on the future, $400 in put time value), but the break-even point would be a futures price of only $364, and the initial out-of-pocket expense would be less. In effect, it would be like buying an insurance policy with a higher deductible.

Just as the amount of protection you desire will affect your choice of a put, so will the length of time you need the protection. The longer you want protection, the more it will cost — i.e., a six-month put will obviously be more expensive to buy than a three-month put. *(NOTE: One long-term option can provide protection on more than one futures purchase. Say you set the strategy in June using December futures and options. In August, prices have risen so you decide to sell the future, continuing to hold the put. Should prices fan and then turn upward again in September, you could once again buy a December futures contract and let the same December option provide the same protection. This is called "trading against an option.")*

Obviously, buying puts to limit losses on long futures positions is a strategy that can be readily tailored to your needs. Indeed, if your tolerance for risk is greater, you can even buy one put for each of two or more long futures positions. With a sharp pencil and the daily option quotes, it's really quite easy to figure out a wide array of risk/reward scenarios involving puts and long futures positions.

I should also mention one other advantage of the Covered Put Purchase over the outright purchase of a call. When you buy a call, that money is spent. It earns no interest and you cannot borrow against its value. However, futures contracts are "marked to the market" every day, meaning your gain or loss is calculated and credited to your account daily. This continuous flow of money into and out of your account can help in meeting margin requirements or averting margin calls.

Now let's see how a covered option strategy works when you're bearish about prices.

Strategy number 12: covered call purchase

ATTITUDE: Extremely bearish.

MOTIVATION: To profit from the expected drop in futures prices while establishing an absolute level of risk.

RISK: Limited to the loss of time value on the option, plus the amount — if any — that the call is out of the money.

PROFIT POTENTIAL: Unlimited. As long as the price of your futures contract continues to decline, your profits will increase, minus only the amount of premium you paid for the protective call.

EXPLANATION OF STRATEGY: You sell a futures contract short and also buy an at-the-money call for the same contract month — i.e., short a December gold futures contract at $360 an ounce and also buy a December $360 gold call. The effect, if you are right, is the same as buying an at-the-money put — if the futures contract moves down in price, you profit fully, minus the premium you paid. If you are wrong, and the futures contract rises, you lose only the time value portion of the premium because the gain in intrinsic value in the call exactly offsets the loss on the short futures contract.

Obviously, the Covered Call Purchase works exactly like the Covered Put Purchase except that is designed to produce profits when prices fall, rather than rise. just to make sure we understand how it works, however, we'll look at one more example.

Graph 13 shows the profit/loss picture in graph form. As you can see, it is the reverse of the Covered Put Purchase graph. The graph

GRAPH 13

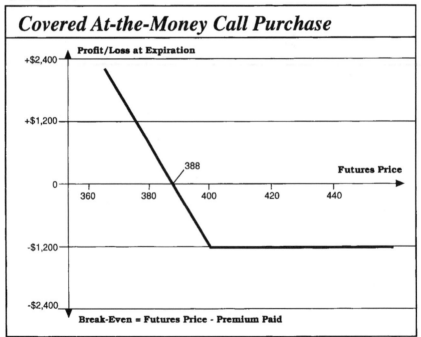

Graph Courtesy of The Commodity Exchange, Inc., New York, NY

assumes the short sale of a gold futures contract at $400 an ounce and the purchase of a $400 gold call at a premium of $12 per ounce.

At any futures price above $400 an ounce, the investor loses money on his short sale, but makes up the loss on his long call. Thus, his maximum loss is the $1,200 premium he paid for the call. On the other hand, as the gold futures price falls below $400, the short sale begins to become profitable while the can loses value. The break even point for the investor is $388 (the short sale price minus the call premium paid). After that, the investor's profit continues to rise as long as the gold futures price falls.

Again, we recommend the use of at-the-money calls in this strategy, but it is possible to do it with other calls if you're willing to accept more risk on the futures contract short sale. In the example above, you could also buy a $420 gold call for, say $5. This would provide less protection since the call would not begin offsetting losses on the short futures contract until the futures price rose above $420, but it would also raise the break-even point. The maximum loss here would be $2,500 ($2,000 on the future, $500 in call time value), but the break even point would be a futures price of only $395. The initial out-of-pocket expense would be less. Again, it would be like buying an insurance policy with a higher deductible.

ADDITIONAL OPTIONS AND FUTURES COMBINATIONS

Options and futures can be used in combination several other ways as well — you can create synthetic straddles for both stable and volatile markets, you can use two options in combination with one futures contract to create synthetic spreads, you can use options to lock in futures profits, and you can use options to add to your profits.

Because we've covered variations of many of these strategies, I won't do a full discussion of each. I would like to close this book, however, by outlining a few of these additional combination uses. I'll start by showing you how to lock in your profits on a long futures position.

Buying puts to lock in profits

This strategy is designed, quite simply, to ensure that you keep the profits you've made in a long futures position.

Assume you bought a December $360 gold futures contract in May and, by August, the price rose to $383. You don't want to sell the contract because you think gold could go still higher — but you don't want to lose your $2,300 in profits if you're wrong. What do you do?

The answer is to lock in the lion's share of your profits by buying a December $380 gold put. Given the current futures price and the time remaining, such a put would probably cost you somewhere in the neighborhood of $5 an ounce, or $500.

What happens then? Should the gold futures contract continue to rise in price, you continue to profit, losing nothing but the $500 you paid for the put. However, should gold begin to drop in price, the put would guarantee that you could never have less than a $1,500 profit. Why? Because the put gives you the right to sell your futures contract at $380 an ounce, no matter how low the futures price goes. Thus, you are guaranteed $2,000 profit on your futures contract, less the

$500 you paid for your put — or $1,500 net profit. Had you remained long the future without buying the put, you would have had no guarantee of any profit at all.

Obviously, the same strategy will work just as well in reverse. If you have substantial unrealized profits on a short futures contract, buying a call near the current price level will protect you against the loss of your profits if the price of the futures contract unexpectedly reverses.

Buying calls to increase profits

One of the most frequently discussed strategies in futures trading is "pyramiding" — the drawing of profits from existing futures positions (remember, the increase in value is credited to your account every day) in order to buy additional futures contracts. For example, assume you deposited $2,000 in margin money and bought a futures contract. If that contract went up in value by $2,000, you could use that unrealized gain as margin to purchase another futures contract. If the two contracts produced $2,000 more in profits, you could buy a third contract, and so on, and so on...

The problem with pyramiding is that it is extremely risky! If prices unexpectedly turn around, an investor who has pyramided into a large number of contracts could find most of his profits wiped out very quickly. With futures options, however, you can accomplish much the same purpose — adding to your profits — with much less risk. Assume you are long two October gold futures contracts at $360 an ounce. The price has moved up to $380, giving you $4,000 in profits. Moreover, you think prices are likely to continue to rise.

You could use the profits to pyramid, buying two more futures contracts (ignore the actual margin requirements for purposes of this example), but if gold prices started going back down you'd have to meet margin calls on four contracts, two of which would be losers.

A better alternative would be to use your $4,000 in gains to buy October $380 gold calls (in using this strategy, you always want to buy the calls closest to the current market price of your profitable futures contract). Let's say those calls we priced at $8. You could buy four calls for a total of $3,200 and still have an $800 cushion in your account for any minor pullbacks.

If gold prices continued to rise, you'd profit on both your futures contracts and on the calls (though the calls would not rise dollar for dollar because of the time value). On the other hand, if prices unexpectedly reversed, your added risk would be only the premium you paid for the calls. In addition, since the calls will retain time value in spite of the falling prices, they will not lose value as fast as extra futures contracts would have.

Obviously, just as you can buy calls to add to a long futures position, you can also use your profits on a short futures position to buy puts, thereby compounding potential gains in downward markets too.

Writing calls against long futures

As I mentioned earlier, futures traders usually have a different definition of 'covered" writing than stock traders. This does not mean, however, that futures traders can't write calls against their long futures positions, Just as stock traders write calls against their long stock positions.

Actually, calls can be written against long futures in a number of ways to accomplish a variety of objectives. For example, calls can be written in an effort to produce a potentially higher selling price and, at the same time, to provide a "cushion" against declines in the futures price. Assume you bought a July sugar futures contract at 10 cents and it subsequently rose to 12 cents, giving you an unrealized profit of $2,240. You don't think there's any danger of sugar prices falling back, but you're also not sure they're going to continue upward. What should you do?

One alternative, of course, would be to simply sell the future and take your profit. The problem with this is that you really feel that sugar could go up another half cent or so and would like the extra profit if it does, especially since you don't see any downside risk.

The other alternative would be to write an at-the-money July 12-cent sugar call and collect the premium — probably somewhere around one-half cent, or $560 on the full 112,000-pound contract. If the futures price does go up, the call will be exercised, making your effective selling price 12.50 cents, just what you hoped to receive (you get 12 cents for selling the futures contract, plus the half-cent you received as a premium on the call). And, if the futures price goes down, the call premium you received will offset the first half-cent of the decline. Thus, if you eventually sold the future at 11.50 cents, your effective selling price (including the option premium), would still be 12 cents — the same amount you would have realized had you sold out in the first place.

The writing of covered calls works best when you feel the market will be steady or slightly bullish. If you were bearish, you'd probably just want to go ahead an sell out your futures position. And, if you were strongly bullish, you wouldn't want to sell a call against your future since such a sale would limit your potential profit to the strike price of the call plus the premium you received.

Buying futures and writing calls

A variation on the above strategy is to buy a futures contract and simultaneously write calls against it rather than waiting to write calls once you have a profit. This variation, called a "buy-and-write" strategy, is closely akin to covered-call writing on stocks since its purpose is to earn an attractive rate of return on the margin investment required to purchase the futures contract. The return, of course, comes from the premium you get when you sell the call.

Assume it's April and the July sugar futures price is 9 cents and requires a margin deposit of $1,000. The July 9-cent sugar call would bring in a premium of $300. You put up the $ 1,000, buy the futures contract, and immediately write the call against it. If the futures price is 9 cents or lower when the can expires, then the call would be worthless and you would get to keep the $300 in premium received. That would give you a 30 percent return on your original $1,000 margin deposit in only three months.

Obviously, this return would be reduced by any loss on the futures contract, so you want to use this strategy only when you feel sure that the market will be stable or very slightly bullish. In our example, a drop of only one-quarter of a cent in the sugar futures price would wipe out your gain on the option premium, so you wouldn't have a lot of downside leeway. Thus, it should be obvious that you cannot just position a buy-and-write strategy and forget it -whenever you write a call against a long futures position you should always plan to watch it very carefully.

A more conservative version of this strategy, applicable to more bullish markets, is to buy futures and write only out-of-the-money calls. This variation appeals to the Banker, the character mentioned earlier in this book. His primary concerns are generally preservation of capital and increased income. He takes the premiums he's paid as a bonus to the profits he makes on his conservative futures strategies or uses them to protect against losses. If a commodity shoots up unexpectedly, he merely lets the futures contract be called away at a small profit. He keeps his premiums and forfeits any gain he would have gotten on the futures contract as a result of its going above the striking price of the out-of-the-money call he sold. He may then look for an alternate commodity to trade, or he may use his profits to fulfill margin requirements and sell naked puts on the same futures contract, waiting until it drops back down in price and then buying it back at the lower price if someone exercises the put.

Again, both of these strategies work just as well in reverse —selling a futures contract short and then writing puts. This is suited to stable or slightly bearish markets, but it's usually not quite as rewarding as covered call writing, simply because, once again, calls generally carry higher premiums than puts.

CONCLUSION

As you have surely figured out, options add a heretofore unavailable flexibility to the world of commodities and futures trading — both in terms of increasing profit opportunities and reducing risk. The strategies I've outlined are the most commonly employed, but there are many more variations which you can structure to meet your needs in virtually any situation.

I hope you've enjoyed this book and — more importantly — I hope that you've learned something that will make you a better and more successful investor in the future. Options on futures are among the newest vehicles in the investment community, but because of their versatility, I feel certain they will prove to be one of the most popular — and potentially rewarding.

Don't miss out on the opportunities they offer!

Tools for Successful Trading

Suggested Reading List

McMillan on Options, *Lawrence G. McMillan,* Almost 600
pages from the world's leading expert on options gives a complete game plan for trading options. Here are McMillan's greatest strategies complete with precise instructions on how and when to use them. It's the definitive source for profitable option players.

570 pp $69.95 Item #T137X-2678

Options as a Strategic Investment, *3rd edition*
Lawrence G. McMillan, It's the top selling options book of all time. Over 800 pages of exhaustive coverage on every aspect of trading options. Called "the single most important options reference available," this mammoth work teaches you to: track volatility and the key role it plays for traders; learn rules for entering/exiting trades at optimal levels, build a successful trading plan. Plus, must-read sections on LEAPS, CAPS, PERCS and cutting edge risk abatement techniques.

884 pp $49.95 Item #T137X-2836

The Option Advisor, *Bernie Schaeffer,* This renowned options
expert reveals the proven wealth-building techniques for selecting the right stocks, assessing risk, managing your options portfolio and—most importantly—for reading market timing indicators. In terms everyone can understand he provides solid ideas on how to use options effectively for conservative and aggressive traders.

316 pp $59.95 Item #T137X-5390

New Option Secret—Volatility, *David Caplan,* Uncovers prac-
tical strategies for using the most important variable in option pricing—volatility –to exploit and profit from the options market. Special section explains how "gurus" like Natenberg, Najarian, Trester and others use volatility to their benefit.

310 pp $65.00 Item #T137X-2889

To order any book listed and receive a special
15% Discount
Call 1-800-272-2855 ext. T137

The New Options Advantage, *David Caplan* — Caplan presents proven strategies that can give you an edge in any market. Read about a no-loss, cost-free hedging method to protect profits, how to recognize and use under/over valued options, how to prevent the most common causes of loss.

245 pp $45.00   Item #T137X-2861

Options for the Stock Investor, *James B. Bittman* — Explains how to use stock options safely and effectively, and how to integrate options into a long-term investment program. Learn time-proven strategies that add value to any investor's portfolio and tactics for investors with varying risk tolerances and goals. Topics include: Basic option strategies, Understanding price behavior, selling options on the stocks you own and using options to achieve long-term goals.

225pp $29.95   Item #T137X-2419

Option Volatility and Pricing Strategies, *Sheldon Natenberg* — Updated new edition tells you how to identify mispriced options and construct volatility and "delta neutral" spreads used by the pros. Using a non-technical trading approach, he leads the reader into the real world of option trading and applies his well developed pricing and volatility theories into practical, tradable strategies.

392 pp $50.00   Item #T137X-3009

Options Essential Concepts & Strategies, *2nd edition, Options Institute* — Expert advice from the "mecca" of options education, the CBOE's Option Institute. Each chapter focuses on a different essential for trading options. Part 1 covers option basics - what they are, how they're priced, how to trade them and pick a strategy. Part 2 contains practical advice for building a trading system - plus when to buy, sell and time trades, and applying the right strategy to current market conditions. The final section, "Real Time Applications" shows how to apply specific indicators to real world case studies.

402 pp $55.00   Item #T137X-2892

To order any book listed and receive a special
15% Discount
Call 1-800-272-2855 ext. T137

The Complete Option Player, *3rd edition*

Ken Trester — Perfect for those get into this market with limited capital, minimal risk and the possibility of spectacular profits. Profitable strategies that exploit little known discrepancies in option pricing, and other cutting edge trading methods - at a great price.

432 pp   Item #T137X-2882 $29.95 **now $15**

DeMark on Day Trading Options: *Using Options to Cash in on the Day Trading Phenomenon, Tom De Mark* —

The first book to combine the excitement of day trading with the continuing and growing popularity of options trading - using DeMark's specially developed indicators and techniques. Discover DeMark's "option trading variable" - the missing link to trading options successfully. Plus, selection best options to day trade, commonly used day trading methods - and more.

358 pp $34.95   Item #T137X-10450

Conservative Investor's Guide to Trading Options

Leroy Gross - Foreword by Larry McMillan — Lots of safe and profitable options strategies for conservative investors. Plus, a full section of aggressive strategies for those willing to take slightly bigger risks. With a new introduction by options guru Larry McMillan, you'll find safe, low risk options methods along with ways to use options as a hedging tool. A great buy.

200 pp $34.95   Item #T137X-10267

Trading Index Options, *James B. Bittman* — Proven techniques
- minus all the math! New Book/Disk combo features the basics of index options - including spreads, how to match strategies with forecasts, alternatives for losing positions, and the importance of price behavior and volatility. Software included provides mulitiple pricing and graphing options.

312 pp $34.95   Item #T137X-2300

Getting Started in Options, *3rd edition, Michael*

Thomsett — This newly updated primer "Demystifies options for the individual investor." Great reference source for pros, and a hands-on starting point for new traders.

291 pp $19.95   Item #T137X-5691

Important Internet Sites

Traders' Library Bookstore — www.traderslibrary.com, the #1 source for trading and investment books, videos and related products.

Essex Trading Company — www.essextrading.com, for important option software products and much more.

Chicago Board of Options Exchange — www.cboe.com, daily market statistics with extensive archives and introduction to options.

Chicago Mercantile Exchange — www.cme.com, market data, live quote services, headlines, etc.

Option Strategist — www.optionstrategist.com, short-term stock and options trading site on the latest techniques and strategies for trading a variety of innovative options products. Free weekly commentary, quotes, volatility data and other tools.

Opportunities in Options — www.oio.com, full service financial services company. Specialists in futures and options.

Optionetics/Option Analysis — www.optionetics.com, market updates, most active gainers/losers, market analysis, Index Charts, research, CMS Bond Quotes, resources and market reports.

Investors Business Daily — www.traderslibrary.com/traders/ibd.cgi, review the latest business news online.

Toronto Stock Exchange — www.tse.com, news services, regulatory changes, the latest publications, newly listed companies, and comments from industry representatives.

Wall Street Directory — www.wsdinc.com, provides access to the best financial sources located throughout the Internet.

Read This Only if You are Serious about Trading Futures or Options

In the late 1980s, the world's financial markets became linked to one another, with price action in one market increasingly affected by the action of related markets. This linking of the financial markets has drastically changed their character and nature, putting previously established methods of single-market analysis to the test. It is no longer sufficient for traders to focus internally on single markets in isolation of what related markets are doing. To be competitive, traders must now have a broad intermarket perspective and the necessary analysis tools to implement it.

Common sense suggests that these correlations between markets have drastically changed the way traders need to do technical analysis. As the linkages between markets became more pronounced in the 1990s and serious traders started to pay attention to them, a new aspect of technical analysis, known as intermarket analysis, has become a critical ingredient to successful trading. Yet, many traders, perhaps the overwhelming majority, are oblivious to these linkages and still ignore *intermarket analysis* - content to limit themselves to analyzing just one market at a time. No wonder such a high percentage of traders lose their money!

The sooner you get on the intermarket bandwagon, the more you'll be able to stack the odds in your favor. There's nothing wrong with single-market analysis; it's just no longer good enough. If you are reasonably successful using your current technical analysis tools, but realize now that you have an intermarket blind spot in your trading arsenal which needs to be corrected, then it's in your own best interest to add intermarket analysis to your trading arsenal before it's too late.

Learn More about
VantagePoint's
Market Timing Technology

VantagePoint will give you a road-map showing you what it expects the market to do, and by doing so will help you build your self-confidence to take trades that should be taken and keep you out of marginal trades that should be avoided.

VantagePoint is ready to use when you receive it, and does not require that you know anything about intermarket analysis or neural networks. You don't need to know anything about programming, unlike other software programs that are so complicated they cause you to take your focus off your trading and get mired and confused dealing with the complexities of the software itself. VantagePoint was designed for use by futures traders who understand that to be successful in today's markets, you need to have a "heads up" on what is *most likely to happen in the market tomorrow,* not just what it has done today or in the past!

VantagePoint *anticipates* trends.
It does not follow them!

Each day you'll know what the trend direction is expected to be over the next two to four days, tomorrow's expected high and low, and whether the market is expected to make a top or a bottom... with a 78% proven accuracy!

What more do you need to be successful?

Call 800-732-5407
www.ProfitTaker.com/60321

This book, along with other books, are available at discounts that make it realistic to provide them as gifts to your customers, clients, and staff. For more information on these long lasting, cost effective premiums, please call John Boyer at 800-424-4550 or email him at john@traderslibrary.com.